The Pan-African Imperative

I0042928

This book argues that the principles of Pan-Africanism are more important than ever in ensuring the liberation of the people of Africa, those at home and abroad, and the rapid development of the African continent.

The writings and practice of Osagyefo Dr. Kwame Nkrumah, Ghana's first post-independence prime minister and president, were key in laying out a vision for post-independence Africa. Now, in an effort to counter the deluge of neo-liberal thinking that has engulfed so much of the debate on African development in recent decades, Michael Williams illuminates just how important a role an Nkrumaist intellectual framework can play in providing an accurate diagnosis of, and effective solution to, Africa's development crisis. This is done by examining Nkrumah's vision of the critical role Pan-Africanism must play in the development of the continent.

Raising vitally important questions about Africa's development and the quality of life of its populations, this book will be a key text for researchers of African politics, development studies, and the Pan-African movement.

Michael Williams recently retired from his position as Academic Director and Professor at Webster University (Ghana Campus). He is the founder of *The Nkrumaist Review: Pan-African Perspectives on African Affairs*, which he edited for ten years.

Routledge African Studies

1. **Oral Literary Performance in Africa**
   Beyond Text
   Edited by Nduka Otiono and Chiji Akọma

2. **Decolonising Childhoods in Eastern Africa**
   Literary and Cultural Representations
   Oduor Obura

3. **The De-Africanization of African Art**
   Towards Post-African Aesthetics
   Edited by Denis Ekpo and Pfunzo Sidogi

4. **Black–Arab Encounters in Literature and Film**
   Touria Khannous

5. **The Pan-African Imperative**
   Revisiting Kwame Nkrumah's Vision for African Development
   Michael Williams

6. **Naming and Othering in Africa**
   Imagining Supremacy and Inferiority through Language
   Sambulo Ndlovu

7. **Memories of Violence in Peru and the Congo**
   Writing on the Brink
   Gilbert Shang Ndi

8. **Black Thought**
   A Theory of Articulation
   Victor Peterson II

For a full list of available titles please visit: https://www.routledge.com/ Routledge-African-Studies/book-series/ROUTAFST

The Pan-African Imperative

Revisiting Kwame Nkrumah's Vision for African Development

Michael Williams

Routledge
Taylor & Francis Group

LONDON AND NEW YORK

First published 2022
by Routledge
2 Park Square, Milton Park, Abingdon, Oxon OX14 4RN

and by Routledge
605 Third Avenue, New York, NY 10158

Routledge is an imprint of the Taylor & Francis Group, an Informa business

British Library Cataloguing-in-Publication Data
A catalogue record for this book is available from the British Library

Library of Congress Cataloging-in-Publication Data
Names: Williams, Michael (Economist), author.
Title: The Pan-African imperative : revisiting Kwame Nkrumah's vision
for African development / Michael Williams.
Description: 1 Edition. | New York, NY : Routledge, 2022. |
Series: Routledge african studies |
Includes bibliographical references and index. |
Identifiers: LCCN 2021033694 (print) | LCCN 2021033695 (ebook) |
ISBN 9781032125183 (hardback) | ISBN 9781032125206 (paperback) |
ISBN 9781003224990 (ebook)
Subjects: LCSH: Nkrumah, Kwame, 1909–1972. | Economic development–Africa. |
Socialism–Africa. | Africa–Politics and government. | Pan-Africanism.
Classification: LCC HC800 .W55 2022 (print) |
LCC HC800 (ebook) | DDC 338.96–dc23
LC record available at https://lccn.loc.gov/2021033694
LC ebook record available at https://lccn.loc.gov/2021033695

ISBN: 978-1-032-12518-3 (hbk)
ISBN: 978-1-032-12520-6 (pbk)
ISBN: 978-1-003-22499-0 (ebk)

DOI: 10.4324/9781003224990

Typeset in Times New Roman
by Newgen Publishing UK

Dedicated to Kwame Ture,
Pan-Africanist *par excellence*,
whose interpretation of Nkrumaism
during the last quarter of the twentieth century,
in theory and in practice, remains the Gold Standard
all revolutionary Pan-Africanists should aspire to emulate.

Contents

Acknowledgements   viii

Introduction   1

1   Historical evolution of Pan-Africanism   5

2   Nkrumaism and radical Pan-African thought   36

3   Continental unification as a prerequisite to African
    development   51

4   Class exploitation and socialist reconstruction in Africa   91

5   Conclusion: political guidelines on achieving a
    unified socialist Africa   127

    Select bibliography   133
    Index   137

Acknowledgements

Numerous friends and colleagues, to whom I am most grateful, have contributed to the final outcome of this book. Their insightful suggestions and recommendations helped to correct errors, mistakes, shortcomings, and misleading statements that I would not have caught without their input. The errors, mistakes, shortcomings, and misleading statements that remain belong to me. However, I must give special thanks to a number people who read significant portions of the manuscript and whose assistance and support served to improve the manuscript significantly. They include Albie Walls, Nii Ardey Otoo, Mjiba Frehiwot, Nehanda Imara, Doreatha Mbalia, Pa Joof, Ama Biney, Salim Faraji, and Jean-Germain Gros. Helena Hurd, Editor of Global Development and African Studies at Routledge Press, provided excellent suggestions that resulted in considerable improvement of the manuscript. I would also like to acknowledge the profound contribution two of my mentors have made to this work, in particular, and to my understanding of Pan-Africanism in general: Dr. Bill Turner, who first introduced Africa to me when I was a 20-year-old kid and nourished my devotion to Pan-Africanism for years afterwards, and Prof. Kofi Asare Opoku, who has helped me to better understand Africa during my past 27 years of living in Ghana. Finally, the consistent support and encouragement provided by my wife, Afua, continues to serve as the foundation upon which I am able to research and write with any degree of competency.

Introduction

Prior to the COVID-19 pandemic, various economic pundits had been lauding the positive economic growth rates of numerous African states.[1] This meant very little for those of us living on the ground. What we have been actually experiencing, then and now, is a continent where the quality of life for the vast majority of its people is arduous, at best, harrowing and dreadful, at worst. This, more than anything else, explains why so many ordinary people have been willing to risk everything, including their very lives on the high seas, to escape. What, after all, is the relevance of economic growth without a commensurate improvement in the living standards of ordinary citizens? If economic growth in Africa is unable to translate into greater access to education, higher life expectancy rates, enhanced environmental protection, increased value added to Africa's raw materials and mineral resources, enduring peace and security, and a significant improvement in the overall quality of human life, what difference does it really matter?

Even the slightest statistical summary reveals a staggering, albeit realistic, picture of what has been taking place in Africa over the past several decades: less than 50 percent of Africa's population has access to hospitals or doctors; close to 1/3 of Africa's population of 1.3 billion lacks access to safe water; the average life expectancy in Africa is less than ten years the global average; 33 percent of the African population suffers from malnutrition; 315 million people in Africa survive on less than $1 per day; one in six children in Africa die before the age of five; only 57 percent of children in Africa are enrolled in primary education; children in Africa account for half of all civilian casualties of wars in Africa; 90 percent of all fatalities caused by malaria in the world occur in Africa, with 80 percent of the victims being children; more than half of Africa's population lives without electricity; nearly 70 percent

DOI: 10.4324/9781003224990-1

of Africa's population depends on biomass—firewood, charcoal, and animal dung—to meet its energy needs for cooking, which destroys the quality of air and the integrity of Africa's forests; Africa is home to 32 of the 38 'Heavily Indebted Poor Countries.' And the statistical litany of this ongoing tragedy, only made worst by COVID-19, could go on *ad infinitum*.[2] We should also note, here, that Africa, a continent of over 1.3 billion people, stretching over 30 million square kilometres of some of the most precious real estate on the planet, has yet to produce a single COVID-19 vaccine, with governments begging for vaccine handouts from whoever will provide them.

All of this, of course, is quite staggering when you consider the potential wealth that could be generated, *for Africa*, from its vast amount of arable land, prodigious labour power, rich mineral resources, and abundant water supply. In short, how, then, can the quality of life for so many in Africa be so dismal? And more importantly, what must be done to ensure Africa's rapid and complete development which, in turn, would contribute to the liberation of Africa and Africans around the world?

It is to these two critical questions that this small book is addressed. And nowhere are these questions addressed more fully than in the thought and practice of Osagyefo Dr. Kwame Nkrumah, the first president of the Republic of Ghana. In an effort to counter the deluge of neo-liberal thinking that has engulfed so much of the debate on matters relating to African development, this study is designed to illuminate just how important a role an Nkrumaist intellectual framework can play in providing an accurate diagnosis of, and effective solution to, Africa's development crisis. This will be done by examining Nkrumah's vision of the critical role Pan-Africanism must play in the development of the continent.

The rational for this approach is based on the following two assumptions. First, the notion of African continental unity must no longer be regarded as if it were anything less than an absolute prerequisite to genuine African development. Nkrumah's warning to Africa that it had but two choices, 'Unite or Perish,' is not as hyperbolic as it sounds. Second, neo-colonial perspectives regarding the merits of so-called free market capitalism, which still befuddle the literature and impact the narrative on African development, continue to camouflage the virulent class struggle that has been waging in Africa long before even the dawn of independence. Hence, how international finance capital, in conjunction with the African elite, serves to impede full-scale industrial development in Africa and, thus, denies ordinary citizens an enhanced quality of life, requires continuous analytical scrutiny. With the use of old *and* new socio-economic mechanisms, the manner in which neo-colonialism serves to block the advance of socialist revolution in Africa necessitates a critical examination. In short, by integrating the analytical concepts of African unification and socialist reconstruction, I have sought to demonstrate just how important an Nkrumaist framework is in helping us to understand and, more importantly, address the critical problems facing Africa and Africans, those at home and abroad.

The relatively recent revival of interest in, and appreciation of, the monumental contributions Nkrumah made to Africa, its people, and the world at-large is encouraging. With Nkrumah having written 15 books, combined with the availability of at least three volumes of his speeches, it is very difficult for most persons who have not read these books to understand the essential ideas that he espoused. In this study, I have sought to glean from these publications, Nkrumah's views on Pan-Africanism as they relate to some of the central issues surrounding African development.

The book begins with a discussion of the historical evolution of the Pan-African movement, a movement that predates not only the European colonial era in Africa, but both the Arab and European slave trades as well. It serves as the foundation upon which the entire discourse is built. Afterwards, an examination of the relationship Nkrumaism shares with radical Pan-African thought is provided. This examination is designed to demonstrate that Nkrumaism represents, first, an ideological reflection of the material conditions of Global Africa and, second, an ideological assimilation, digestion, advancement, and refinement of radical Pan-African thought that preceded and surrounded Nkrumah during his lifetime. The main purpose of this chapter is to illustrate that we are not talking about the intellectual landscape of just one man, but rather the embodiment, in thought and action, of what has evolved over centuries in the lives of African people, those at home and those abroad. The study then examines, in two subsequent chapters, the two main pillars of Pan-Africanism advocated by Nkrumah in his writings and speeches: a united Africa and socialist revolution. The concluding chapter rests on a brief discussion of the political measures needed, outlined in various Nkrumaist texts, to achieve the goals of Pan-Africanism.

This book is not designed to explore, challenge, confirm, criticize, or reject any of the various theoretical schools of thought, old or new, on matters related to African development. As interesting as such a study would be, this is not the aim of this work. Instead, the sole purpose of this book is to analyze some of the major challenges of development facing Africa from an Nkrumaist perspective.

Notes

1 Steven Radelet, *Emerging Africa: How 17 Countries Are Leading the Way*, London: Center for Global Development, 2010; Jonathan Berman, *Success in Africa: CEO Insights from a Continent on the Rise*, Brookline, MA: Bibliomotion, 2013;Vijay Mahajan, *Africa Rising: How 900 Million African Customers Offer More Than You Think*, Upper Saddle River, NJ: Prentice Hall, 2009; OECD/AFDB/UNDP, *African Economic Outlook 2014: Global Value Chains and Africa's Industrialisation*, OECD Publishing, Paris, 2014; Edward Miguel, *Africa's Turn?*, Cambridge, MA: MIT Press, 2009.
2 UNDP, 'Africa: Latest Human Development Index Shows Overall Slowdown in Growth,' July 24, 2014: http://allafrica.com/stories/20140 7241646.html; UNDP, *Africa Human Development Report, 2012: Towards a Food Secure Future*, New York: United Nations Publications, 2012; C.P. Emenike et al., eds. 'Accessing Safe Drinking Water in Sub-Saharan Africa: Issues and Challenges in South-West Nigeria,' In *Sustainable Cities and Society*, Amsterdam: Elsevier, 2017, pgs. 263–272; African Studies Centre, Leiden, 'Water in Africa,' Retrieved from: www.ascleiden.nl/content/webdossiers/water-africa; Hannah Ritchie and Max Roser, 'Clean Water,' Our World in Data, 2019, Retrieved from: https://ourworldindata.org/water-access; Danwood M. Chirwa, 'Access to Medicines and Health Care in Sub-Saharan Africa: A Historical Perspective,' *Maryland Journal of International Law*, Vol. 31, No. 1, 2017, pgs. 21–43; Max Roser et al., 'Life Expectancy,' *Our World of Data*, 2019, Retrieved from: https://ourworldindata.org/life-expectancy; Aaron O'Neill, 'Life Expectancy in Africa from 1950 to 2020, *Statista*, 2019, Retrieved from: www.statista.com/statistics/1076271/life-expectancy-africa-historical/; WHO, *Nutrition in the WHO African Region*, World Health Organization, Regional Office for Africa, Brazzaville, 2017; World Bank, The World by Income and Region, World Development Indicators, 2021, Retrieved from: https://datatopics.worldbank.org/world-development-indicators/the-world-by-income-and-region.html; UNDP, 'Africa: Latest Human Development Index Shows Overall Slowdown in Growth,' July 24, 2014: http://allafrica.com/stories/201407241 646.html; UNDP, *Africa Human Development Report, 2012: Towards a Food Secure Future*, New York: United Nations Publications, 2012.

1 Historical evolution of Pan-Africanism

Definition

While the definition of Pan-Africanism, like the movement itself, has evolved over time, much of what it means today is what it meant centuries earlier: the collective movement of African people towards unity, independence, and liberation. This movement has expressed itself in small-scale to large-scale endeavours, in short periods to periods of much longer duration, and from one part of the globe to another. It has also incorporated a wide spectrum of human behaviour. This has included either a sole reliance on, or a combination of, various political, economic, religious, and cultural activities. Although never centrally coordinated, the Pan-African movement, in its broadest terms, has been, and continues to be, a movement of people of African descent working together, often across ethnic and geopolitical boundaries, to unify and liberate Africa and Africans everywhere.

However, today, after, and in response to more than 500 years of Africa's entanglement with European insufficiency and capitalist expansionism, viz., slavery, colonialism and neo-colonialism, the Pan-African movement has evolved into a variant of the international socialist movement as well. In other words, the struggle to emancipate Africa and its people, those at home and abroad, has become an integral part of the universal struggle between capital and labour, that is, between the owners of the means of production and the workers of the world, whose labour power produces the fruit upon which the owners depend in their unbridled accumulation of wealth. In fact, nearly all of the leading advocates of Pan-Africanism during most of the twentieth century, and beyond, have either been socialists or, like Malcolm X, heavily attracted to an economic system that would ensure an equitable distribution of socially produced wealth.[1] After all, the plight of the slave, his colonial brother, and the modern proletariat is much the same: their labour

DOI: 10.4324/9781003224990-2

power is exploited to enhance the wealth of a rich minority. This is why Nkrumah was able to surmise that 'Capitalism is but the gentleman's method of slavery.'[2] George Padmore, C.L.R. James, W.E.B. Du Bois, Shirley Graham Du Bois, Julius Nyerere, John Henrik Clarke, Robert Sobukwe, Modibo Keita, Ahmed Sékou Touré, Ahmed Ben Bella, Cheik Anta Diop, Frantz Fanon, Eslanda Robeson, Amilcar Cabral, Patrice Lumumba, Kwame Ture, Thomas Sankara, Muammar Qadhafi, and Kwame Nkrumah are just some of the important Pan-African socialists who, through their thought and action, helped to define the movement as we know it today.

Even the legendary Pan-Africanist, Marcus Garvey, who has been unfairly chided, by some, for being a so-called black capitalist, was not only very sympathetic to the 1917 Bolshevik revolution[3]; he also constantly spoke about the need for egalitarianism, equal opportunity, and true brotherhood within the global African community. These notions were particularly important to him whenever he spoke of bringing Africans from different parts of the world together for resettlement in Africa.[4] In short, Garvey's allegiance to the aspirations of African workers, from his years in Jamaica before arriving in Harlem until his final years in London, was unwavering. Instead, what often gets mistaken as his opposition to socialism was his battle with so-called socialists themselves, black and white, who, out of jealousy, envy, and ideological disparity, were bent on destroying Garvey, the Universal Negro Improvement Association (UNIA), and his fiercely Pan-African movement.[5]

In short, the highest definition of Pan-Africanism remains, to date, the Nkrumaist ideological embodiment of what Nkrumah, his contemporaries, and their predecessors bequeathed to their descendants in the fight against the exploitation and domination of Africa by international finance capital: one, unified, socialist Africa, that is, the United States of Africa, self-reliant and free of any variant of racial and ethnic oppression, gender domination, and class exploitation. As Nkrumah noted years ago, 'Socialism and [African] unity are organically complementary.'[6] This, in fact, was the exact prescription W.E.B. Du Bois, the so-called 'Father of Pan-Africanism,' gave to the delegates at the 'All African People's Conference' held in Accra in December 1958: 'Awake Africa! Put on the beautiful robes of Pan-African socialism. You have nothing to lose but your chains! You have freedom and dignity to attain!'[7] Nothing has happened since then, including the onerous burden of an ascending globalization, that would warrant Pan-Africanism being redefined or taking a different course from that which has been crystallized by its progenitors. Indeed, this study is designed to demonstrate that there is no other way that Africans, at home and abroad, can achieve their complete liberation.

Origin

The roots of Pan-Africanism lie squarely in Africa. For too long historians, and even Pan-Africanists themselves, have traced the movement to unite the continent and its people to the transatlantic slave trade or, sometimes later, to the Pan-African Conference held in London in July 1900.[8] This meeting, organized by Henry Sylvester Williams of Trinidad, is often credited with putting the word 'Pan-Africanism' in the dictionary. Then, nearly two decades later, Du Bois—who actually attended the 1900 London conference—began organizing a series of Pan-Africanist Congresses in 1919. The most significant of these congresses, the fifth, was held in Manchester, England, in 1945 under the leadership of Padmore and Nkrumah.[9] These formal gatherings, and lest we forget the brilliant conventions organized in Harlem by Garvey and his UNIA during the early 1920s, represent a cherished legacy in the struggle to unite Africa and its scattered and suffering people.[10]

However, this was not the beginning. After all, even Williams was busy organizing fellow Africans from different parts of the world—to give them an independent voice in resisting the oppression that had engulfed them—into his *African Association* in the last quarter of the nineteenth century.[11] And more than a century earlier, we have documented evidence of displaced Africans, slaves in New England (USA), struggling to re*unite* with the motherland.[12] Indeed, the efforts of countless numbers of Africans in the Diaspora to return home, discussed below, constitute an integral part of the Pan-Africanist movement as well, the tragic and anomalous histories of early statehood in Liberia and Sierra Leone notwithstanding.[13]

Instead, it seems far more accurate to argue that the movement to unite Africa and its people, which represents the very epitome of Pan-Africanism, began somewhere in the long centuries before foreign invaders entered Africa and changed its course. During this pre-invasion period in Africa, we have a near steady progression of smaller and weaker ethnic formations being swallowed up by, and integrated into, larger, stronger, and more developed ethnic and regional formations as part of the process of creating huge nation-states. This evolutionary, Pan-African process is, in fact, what the slave traders, from both the east and the west, and later European imperialism served to arrest. Two relatively modern and glaring examples of this process took place amongst the expansionist empires of the Asante in West Africa and the Zulu in

Southern Africa—both of which were brutally dismantled by British imperialism.[14] But they were not the only ones. Once again, this process was taking place in several regions throughout the continent, so much so that it would not be difficult to argue, or to at least honestly speculate, the following: had Africa not suffered from these external invasions, the number of nation-states in Africa, currently, would hardly reach 10, let alone the 55 artificially created ones we have today.

Before the invasions, the economic, political, and cultural interactions between the various regions and peoples of Africa were characterized by absorption, immersion, assimilation, domination, and integration.[15] This process, not unlike what took place in much of the world outside of Africa, was shaped largely by the wide variety and similarity of Africa's topography and geography, and the normal socio-cultural vicissitudes that occur when people struggle to adapt, survive, and flourish in the physical environment and social milieu that they meet. This same process helps to explain why precolonial African cultural patterns, throughout much of the continent, share so much in common, especially in matters relating to familial life, governance, health care, agriculture, linguistic structure, artistic expression, and the philosophical concepts of time, space, and being.[16]

Although this movement in Africa was not conscious of itself, unlike modern social movements (with their stated programmes, agendas, and objectives), this informal human activity should not cloud our understanding of where Africa was headed: family, clan, tribe, nation, and continent, in short, Pan-Africanism—before, that is, European imperialism fossilized Africa at the tribal stage while balkanizing the entire continent into the factitious, fragmented, warring mess it is today.

Early emigration efforts

As stated earlier, an integral part of the Pan-African movement during its pre-twentieth-century phase included experiences that resulted from the forced, violent removal of countless millions of Africans from the African mainland to the plantations of North, South, and Central America and the Caribbean islands. Not only were there communities and leaders, *in Africa,* who fought against this grave human tragedy, there was also a vast community of stolen Africans, dispersed throughout the Western Hemisphere, who sought every means possible to return to the African motherland. This struggle began in earnest during the earliest years of slavery. Not only did the lyrics of songs sung by Africans during this period, in both North America and the Caribbean, indicate a strong desire to reunite with Africa; even attempted suicides often reflected their longing to return home (specifically to the ancestral abode).[17] This rudimentary manifestation of Pan-African consciousness among enslaved Africans and their emancipated brethren continued throughout the slave period. In fact, it continued for many decades after slavery, albeit at different levels of momentum and with different degrees of success. As would be expected, this longstanding interest among the displaced Africans of the Americas in physically returning to Africa was greater among those who were most oppressed and/or who felt the most excluded from Western Hemispheric institutions.

The repatriation experiences of Africans in the Diaspora who returned to West Africa during the nineteenth century to establish Sierra Leone and Liberia are often included as part of the historical evolution of Pan-Africanism. However, these experiences were more anomalous to, than congruent with, the historical evolution of the Pan-African movement. Both states became, *in effect*, colonies of Great Britain and the United States, respectively (although Liberia was, technically, independent). And with the assistance of a class of educated, privileged, and financially advantaged African descendants from abroad, the indigenous populations were compelled to provide exploitable labour for foreign capitalist investments.[18]

Still, the willingness of thousands of Africans in the Americas and Western Europe to return to Africa—*albeit arranged under white tutelage*—is an indication of the strong Pan-African sentiments among the scattered descendants of Africa at that time and long afterwards. Moreover, many emigration movements, organizations, and leaders that emerged after the founding of Sierra Leone, and especially of Liberia, often centred their efforts around the existence and symbolic nature of these two states.

As an alternative to the white-dominated emigration schemes of groups like the American Colonization Society, which transported thousands of Africans in North America to Liberia, there were many black-dominated efforts to reunite the African Diaspora with the African mainland.[19] This activity also represented a genuine sentiment and burgeoning interest in Pan-African unity. As early as 1773, slaves in New England petitioned the Massachusetts colonial legislature to be emancipated in order that they may return to Africa. During this same time, Africans from Jamaica, who were exiled by Great Britain to Canada, were organizing themselves around identical requests to their European captors. In the Caribbean, men such as Cinque in Cuba and Daaga in Trinidad led movements in the 1830s to reunite with Africa. The wealthy New England shipping merchant, Paul Cuffe, whose father was from the Akan-speaking peoples of Ghana, is often credited with organizing the first successful attempt to return Africans in the Diaspora back to Africa. Having done so in 1815, Cuffe died unexpectedly two years later. Had he lived longer he may have achieved even greater success, given his financial strength and the genuine support his plans received from the population of 'free' blacks at that time.

By 1859, Robert Campbell of Jamaica and Martin Delaney of the United States travelled to Africa, together, in search for land for resettlement purposes. They succeeded in signing an agreement with a Yoruba King that gave them and their followers the rights to uncultivated land. The advent of the Civil War in the United States, however, was among other factors that prevented Delaney and Campbell from realizing their Pan-African goals. One year before Delaney and Campbell travelled to Africa, Henry Highland Garnet founded, and became president of, the African Civilization Society. While his organization, like others before and after it, had 'civilizing' ambitions that reflected the Eurocentric biases of the nineteenth and twentieth centuries, it also had aims that were both militant and Pan-African. In addition to seeking to 'strike the deathblow to American slavery,' one of its major objectives in Africa was 'to establish a grand centre of negro nationality, from which shall flow the streams of commercial, intellectual, and political power which shall make colored people respected everywhere.'[20] Despite his occasional vacillation, Garnet succeeded in keeping alive the notion of reunification with Africa. Still, he was unable to implement his plans effectively, partly because of the hostility he received from men such as Frederick Douglass in the United States who adamantly opposed any efforts that were inconsistent with his aspirations for black assimilation into the North American mainstream.

During this same period in the Caribbean and Latin America, there were many African descendants who sought and advocated a return to Africa in order to assist in the continent's development. Although they mostly came as Christian missionaries, these black missionaries had motives that were often significantly different from their European counterparts, the latter of whom often worked in concert with European explorers and colonizers.[21] One of the groups responsible for organizing this trek of black missionaries from the Caribbean to Africa was the West Indian Church Association, formed in the 1850s. One of the most successful products of this effort was Edward Wilmot Blyden from St. Thomas, in the Virgin Islands, who began his evolution into Pan-Africanism as a Christian missionary. After dropping this pursuit, Blyden, based largely in Liberia and Sierra Leone, soon became one of the leading Pan-African intellectuals in the African World. Throughout the last quarter of the nineteenth century, he worked laboriously for

African descendants in the Diaspora to return home and contribute to Africa's development. Due largely to his encouragement, many other African descendants in the Caribbean sought to return home. Moreover, through his writings and teaching, Blyden was able to influence countless Pan-Africanists of the early twentieth century that followed in his footsteps, for example, Du Bois, Garvey, Padmore (who named his daughter, Blyden), and the great Pan-Africanist, J.E. Casely Hayford (of the 'Gold Coast'). Hayford became a disciple of Blyden when the former attended school at Fourah Bay College in Sierra Leone, where Blyden was located, in the last quarter of the nineteenth century.[22]

African missionaries from the United States were also actively involved in traveling to Africa and spending long periods of interaction with their mainland kinfolk. Some even became renowned for the important contributions they were making to Africa.[23] However, the impact this experience was having in the United States also had important Pan-African implications. Historian John Hope Franklin once wrote about this impact:

> their presence in Africa had a profound and lasting effect on Negroes in the United States. It kept alive their interest in Africa. As missionaries returned and told of their experiences, as they sought continued support of their overseas enterprises, as they underscored the continued cultural, racial, and even political bonds between Negro Americans and Africans, they convinced many Negro Americans that Africa was indeed worthy of their interest and consideration.[24]

One important variant of the emigration phase of pre-twentieth-century Pan-Africanism was created by the independence of Haiti in 1804. In fact, the tremendous contribution Haiti has made to the Pan-African movement continues to be significantly neglected in our understanding of the contribution of the African Diaspora to African unity, independence, and liberation.[25] Not only did Haiti's first constitution ban slavery on the island; it also granted freedom and Haitian citizenship to any enslaved African who escaped to its shores. Furthermore, its first leader, Jean-Jacques Dessalines, not only threatened to invade Jamaica to end slavery there, but also threatened to 'mount a naval expedition back to Africa in order to stop the slave trade at its source.'[26] For these reasons, Haiti, almost as much as Africa, represented a Pan-African destination for those Africans in the Diaspora seeking to escape European domination during much of the nineteenth century. Haiti also provided a core of exceptional Pan-African leaders—Joseph-Antenor

Firmin, Benito Sylvain, and Jean Price-Mars, among others—whose contributions, though largely unknown by English speakers, have been well documented.[27]

During the last decade of the nineteenth century, no one better embodied the notion that oppressed descendants of Africa, especially in the United States, should return to Africa in order to help liberate Africa and Africans everywhere than Bishop Henry McNeal Turner. He was a leader in the African Methodist Episcopal Church in the United States and engaged in various efforts to realize his Pan-African goals. Turner made frequent trips to Africa and constantly promoted the idea of African emigration in response to the growing disenchantment among the poorer segments of the African population in the United States. Poor black landless peasants, recently freed from chattel slavery, but living under the most virulent forms of racial terrorism, were especially receptive to Turner's message. Although he, too, never succeeded in transporting a significant number of people back to Africa, he did make a significant contribution towards keeping certain fundamental Pan-African ideals alive. Foremost among these was the notion that the only hope for scattered African descendants was in building a powerful and independent African nation.

There were many other emigration efforts that took place in different parts of the African World during this period, and for the exact same reason: oppressed, displaced Africans saw their liberation indelibly linked with returning to the African motherland. The Tabon from Bahia in northeast Brazil, who travelled to, and permanently settled in, various communities in West Africa readily come to mind.[28] However, a genuine appreciation of this particular dimension of the historical evolution of Pan-Africanism requires an understanding of several key points. First, the black controlled efforts never made claims on land outside or inside of Africa that required the political subjugation, economic exploitation, or eventual expulsion of indigenous inhabitants. Second, the majority of followers of these movements belonged to the poorer, excluded segments of the societies where they lived, as the more economically mobile often observed with disdain. Third, in relative terms, while the number of African descendants who actually returned to Africa was never large, these figures belie the actual support that emigration schemes received from the masses of scattered, displaced Africans.[29] Fourth, these movements, although never really anti-capitalist in their ideological orientation, were clearly a part of the resistance to the consolidation of black suffering under the systematic transition from capitalism proper to colonial imperialism. This is why these movements—fostered, sheltered, and endured by their white patrons *before* the 'Scramble for Africa'—were vehemently opposed by the turn of the twentieth century. By then an aggressive imperialism was unwilling to tolerate any 'outside interference.' And fifth, these movements were very influential in the historical development of Pan-Africanism. In short, they became effectively interwoven with similar and new movements and events that occurred in the struggle for Pan-African unity during the twentieth century and beyond.

Early twentieth-century developments

Pan-African activity geared towards physically reuniting African descendants abroad with their ancestral homeland did not stop after the turn of the century. Bishop Turner continued to lead the emigration movement in the United States during the first decade of the new century. Replacing the void left by Turner after his death was Chief Alfred Sam of the Gold Coast in West Africa. However, Chief Sam succeeded in returning only a small amount of followers to the Gold Coast. This was due partly because of the conditions of underdevelopment in Africa, and partly because of the intransigence of British colonial authorities, especially emigration officials, who frustrated Chief Sam and his followers at every turn.[30]

The evangelical dimension of the Pan-African struggle to return African descendants home also continued. These efforts contributed in no small way to the radicalization of the religious leadership and laity in Africa.[31] As a consequence, by 1926, white missionaries—the religious embodiment of European expansionism in Africa—grew so disquieted from the growing Africanization and radicalization of Euro-Christian doctrines that they organized, in Le Zoute, Belgium, an international conference of missionaries concerned with Africa. One of the main purposes of this conference was to prevent the migration of black missionaries whose teachings, they felt, resulted in 'serious disturbances' in Africa.[32]

Although the European partitioning and colonization of Africa began nearly two decades before the beginning of the new century (formalized at the infamous Berlin Conference of 1884–1885), it was not completed until two decades into the twentieth century (resulting from post-WWI reconfigurations). As mentioned earlier, this led to a decline in the *emigration* phase of pre-twentieth-century Pan-Africanism. However, this void was quickly filled with the emergence of the *organizational* phase of Pan-African resistance to the plundering of Africa. Already, prior to the twentieth century, a considerable amount of communication and interaction had taken place between Africans on the mainland and their brethren scattered abroad.[33] It is no wonder, then, that African descendants in different parts of the world were able to pull themselves together, organizationally, into various Pan-African associations during the first quarter of the twentieth century to fight against the advances of European hegemony in Africa. Du Bois had been advocating this for years. 'When once the blacks of the United States, the West Indies, and Africa work and think together,' he wrote, 'the future of the black man in the modern world is safe.'[34] And so, as mentioned earlier, several conferences, congresses, and conventions were organized by Africans, globally, some even before the twentieth century. Their *raison d'etre* was simple: to address the common misery and suffering being superimposed on Africa and Africans, everywhere, in this new era. Some of the most important gatherings of this type included the Pan-African Conference of 1900 in London; the Pan-Africanist Congresses inspired and organized by Du Bois between 1919 and 1927 in different European capitals and New York City; and Garvey's UNIA conventions that met in the Harlem between 1920 and 1925.

On the mainland, a variant of this same effort materialized. To regain the land and power violently usurped by the colonial powers, organized resistance emerged everywhere. In West Africa, Casely Hayford took the lead. In 1920 he and other West African nationalists formed the National Congress of British West Africa (NCBWA).[35] And interestingly enough, they did so by transcending ethnic ties and colonial state configurations in pursuit of larger nation-state ambitions. In fact, the original conveners of NCBWA had envisioned their organization as the initial phase of a Union of West African States.[36] But there were countless others. The Maji Maji Rebellion in Tanganyika, the East African Association in Kenya, peasant revolts in Madagascar, and protracted rebellions in Somalia were just some of the resistance movements that multiplied across the continent and, often, across tribal lines. However, the British and their European counterparts, including the Germans before WWI, consistently used every means available— legal and extralegal—to dismantle, frustrate, or destroy these trans-ethnic, Pan-African associations in Africa.[37] During this same period, even radical clerics who found ways to use the bible *and* indigenous cultural beliefs to oppose colonial rule faced the same wrath. The 1915 rebellion of Reverend John Chilembwe and his followers in Nyasaland, who invoked Garvey's most famous mantra, 'Africa for the Africans,' serves as a painful reminder of just how far colonial rule was prepared to squash these Pan-African uprisings.[38]

During this period, the bourgeois 'freedoms' that prevailed in the industrial countries, primarily of assembly and of speech, account for why Africans in the Diaspora were able to organize their resistance more freely than their counterparts in the colonies. Though carefully scrutinized (and plotted against) by the intelligence community of their respective countries,[39] Africans in the United States and western Europe were not only able to hold more meetings, above ground, than their colonial brethren; they were also able to build organizations and institutions that were less transient and more globally recognized than those built under the repressive climate of colonial Africa. Their access to the means of mass communications, alone, meant that they could reach millions more people than their kinfolk in Africa. This activity resulted in a plethora of gatherings that were attended by outstanding Pan-African proponents as well as other notable intellectuals, business people, bureaucrats, and royalty within the African World. Although reformist in nature (save for most of Garvey's proclamations), the resolutions drafted at these meetings shared consistent themes and demonstrated a common Pan-African awareness of the conditions facing global Africa in the first quarter of the twentieth century. They encouraged greater Pan-African cooperation between peoples of African descent; decried the technological and industrial underdevelopment that was crippling Africa's future under colonial rule; championed the sovereignty of the only three black independent republics in the world at that time: Haiti, Liberia, and Ethiopia; sought ways to pressure the European powers to relinquish their political hold on Africa in favour of African self-government; and remained consistently anti-imperialist, although varying in tone depending on a given organization's ideological outlook. It is worth noting that despite efforts to hold some of these meeting on African soil, the imperialist powers consistently refused to allow this to ever happen. This also explains why even holding a copy of the UNIA newspaper, the *Negro World*, was decreed a seditious act in most of colonial Africa and the Caribbean.[40]

In fact, the achievements of Marcus Garvey and his UNIA and African Communities League (UNIA-ACL) deserve special attention. In the long history of Pan-Africanism, few, if any, can rival the contributions UNIA-ACL made to this movement.[41] Garvey, along with his first wife, Amy Ashwood Garvey, founded the UNIA in Jamaica in 1914. He did so, according to his own account, to address the wretched condition of the African World at that time—much of which he observed, first hand, through his travels. Furthermore, Garvey benefitted from, and was deeply influenced by, the Pan-African efforts of his nineteenth century and early twentieth century predecessors.[42] With chapters and divisions of the UNIA in almost every corner of the African World, Garvey could boast of a membership of nearly six million. With great organizational effort and oratorical skill, Garvey took advantage of the frustrations and disillusionment that African descendants were experiencing after WWI. Having fought and died, supposedly, to make the world safe for democracy, African veterans returned to domiciles that were as racist as they were before the war. Africans, especially those in the United States who were migrating to urban centres in the south and the north, grew extremely angry and bitter, especially in light of the frequency of race riots that were dotting the American urban landscape. The false expectations that life would be better, along with the denial of basic human rights, provided just the right fuel for Garvey's brand of Pan-Africanism to succeed. And it did, in practically every large community where Africans, mainly in the Diaspora, were located.

The Garvey programme, despite its limitations, addressed many of the basic problems—material and immaterial—that confronted Global Africa. Still, most historians and other commentators have consistently and mistakenly reduced Garveyism to simply a 'Back to Africa' movement.' However, although emigration plans were undoubtedly a part of the UNIA's overall scheme, its primary and ultimate objective was to wrestle Africa from the clutches of European imperialism in order to build it into a nation powerful enough to liberate Africans around the world. No one said it better than Garvey himself:

> We are determined to solve our own problem, by redeeming our Mother-Land Africa from the hands of alien exploiters and found there a Government, a nation of our own, strong enough to lend protection to the members of the race scattered all over the world, and to compel the respect of the nations and races of the earth.[43]

Having lionized some of the most fundamental ideals of the Pan-African movement like never before, there is little wonder why the imperialist powers had such a keen interest in seeing Garvey fail.

It was also the Garvey movement which served to highlight the invaluable role played by African women in the Pan-African movement.[44] For while African women, as ordinary 'foot soldiers,' were always an integral part of every historical period in the Pan-African movement, it was during this *organizational* phase, and especially in the Garvey movement itself, that their contributions became more prominent and, thus, better documented. We could begin by mentioning the critical roles played by both of Garvey's wives in the earlier and later stages of the UNIA's development in particular, and in the Pan-African cause in general. Amy Ashwood and Amy Jacques, both with strong feminist credentials, were formidable organizers and propagandists throughout their adult lives, including the periods when they were no longer at Garvey's side.[45] Amy Ashwood, a multi-talented, renaissance woman, travelled extensively, including long stints in West Africa. She spent the larger part of her adult life giving speeches and helping to build Pan-African organizations in the United States, the Caribbean, and Europe. With Amy Jacques, while the majority of her organizational activity was absorbed in helping build the UNIA, it was as a wordsmith for the *Negro World* and other publications where she made an indelible mark as a dedicated Pan-Africanist freedom fighter.[46]

Additionally, there was a community of other important female leaders within the UNIA who deserve special attention, including Emily Christmas Kinch, Carrie Mero Leadett, Mary E. Johnson, Janie Jenkins, Marie Duchaterlier, Irena Moorman Blackston, Sarah Branch, Maymie Leona Turpeau De Mena, Georgiana O'Brien, Elinor Robinson White, and the extremely talented Henrietta Vinton Davis, the latter of whom, for years, served as second in command to Garvey himself.[47] However, more important than the individual female contributions to the UNIA's development was the collective contribution made to the organization by the majority of its women: they laboured, diligently, inside the organization to help it meet its Pan-African objectives. The role played by the Black Cross Nurses, a female auxiliary of the UNIA, was a perfect example. Formed in cities throughout the United States, Canada, Central America, and the Caribbean, these women provided a huge boost towards the realization of Pan-African aims. With formal medical training, or with practical training in First Aid and nutrition, these women—providing much needed community work in public health and infant and home care—went very far in helping to materialize the Pan-African objective of self-reliance and independence.

At the end of WWI, in addition to the Garvey movement, there emerged a large number of other significant Pan-African activities taking place among colonial subjects living in Western Europe.[48] While some of these activists received their initial impetus from the Garvey movement, many of them arose out of the same contradictions that produced Garvey's followers: the disenchantment with a colonial society, after risking life and limb on the battlefields of war torn Europe, which provided little or no opportunity to prosper or to enjoy democratic rights. These activities centred around the creation of several organizations dedicated to the realization of Pan-African aims. In London, Africans from West Africa and the Caribbean formed the Union for Students of African Descent in 1917. A year later, also in London, the African Progress Union (APU) was formed. The famous Egyptian Pan-Africanist, Duse Mohamed Ali, was one of its members.

The APU's declared aim was to promote the social and economic welfare of African peoples throughout the world. By the mid-1920s the influential West African Student Union (WASU) was established. Despite its name, the membership of WASU included Africans from different parts of the African World besides West Africa. Indeed, WASU's very origin owed much to the organizational efforts of Amy Ashwood Garvey.[49] Moreover, it was not concerned with just student-related issues, but with matters affecting the entire African World.

France, having expropriated more African land than any other European nation, was not devoid of this same Pan-African activity after WWI. In addition to its capital serving as the location of the first Pan-Africanist Congress of 1919, the Paris Peace Conference in Versailles, held during the same period, was the target of further Pan-African activity.[50] Du Bois, Garvey, and other notable Pan-African figures sought to arrange for Africa to have a voice at this Conference. Besides advocating for the establishment of a Charter of Human Rights to guide the colonial powers in their relations with mainland Africa, they sought to affect the impending redivision of Africa by the victorious Allied Powers along lines consistent with their Pan-African goals. That the European powers chose to ignore these concerns and continue pursuing their imperialist agenda in Africa should not overshadow the significance of this Pan-African appeal. Indeed, subsequent to this, not only did Du Bois make similar *requests* to the newly formed League of Nations, but Garvey and the UNIA made identical *demands* to this same body.

The French-speaking African community in France built several Pan-African organizations in Paris. Men such as Prince Kojo Tovalou Houenou of Dahomey, founder and president of the *Ligue Universelle pour la Defense de la Race Noire*, challenged the assimilationist policies of French colonialism between the years of 1924 and 1936. Interestingly, Houenou, an associate of Garvey, was invited to attend the 1924 UNIA Convention in New York City. With the production of its journal, *Les Continents*, the *Ligue Universelle* pursued aims that were quintessentially Pan-African. Also important during this period was the *Comite de la Defense de la Race Negre*, led by Lamine Senghor from Senegal, and the *Ligue de la Defense de la Race Negre*, led by Tiemoho Garon Koyate from the Sudan. These two organizations, built by French-speaking African descendants from Africa and the Caribbean, showed great interest in the plight of the African Diaspora in the United States and were particularly impressed with the rise of Garveyism. Moreover, they were more radical than the *Ligue Universelle* as they understood, and criticized, vehemently, the collaboration between the rulers of French colonialism and the French-speaking, African middle class. Consequently, they earned a considerable amount of hostility from French government authorities.

The ideological radicalization of the Pan-African movement continued during the 1930s in Great Britain. Led by African descendants who were mainly from the Caribbean, numerous Pan-African organizations were established by committed socialists.[51] George Padmore and C.L.R. James, friends from childhood in Trinidad, readily come to mind. During the 1930s, James formed the International African Friends of Abyssinia (IAFA). Shortly afterwards, Padmore established the International African Service Bureau (IASB), which was replaced by the Pan-African Federation in 1944. James and Padmore, along with other West Indians, were joined by other notable activists from different parts of Africa, for example, Jomo Kenyatta of Kenya, I.T.A. Wallace-Johnson of Sierra Leone, and Peter Abrahams of South Africa. Collectively, through the convening of several meetings and the dissemination of anti-colonial writings, they were responsible for maintaining one of the most significant bases of Pan-African opposition to imperialist plunder in the world. George Padmore—soon to become Nkrumah's most important ideological mentor—was especially prodigious in this account.[52] And while the ideological persuasion of this group of Pan-Africanists was diverse, they were all heavily influenced by the writings of Karl Marx and V.I. Lenin, and the tumultuous events that emanated from the Great October Revolution of 1917.

In October of 1935, the Italian invasion of Ethiopia intensified the growing anti-imperialist orientation of the Pan-African movement. As chairman of the IAFA, James' outcry to this invasion reflected the views of many Pan-Africanists during this period:

> Africans and people of African descent, especially those who have been poisoned by British Imperialist education, needed a lesson. They have got it. Every succeeding day shows exactly the real motives which move Imperialism in its contact with Africa, shows the incredible savagery and duplicity of European Imperialism in its quest for markets and raw materials.[53]

In various countries around the world, the Pan-African response was immense.[54] Africans mobilized Ethiopian support groups, raised funds for weapons and medical supplies, boycotted Italian-produced goods, wrote articles condemning Italy and admonishing the League of Nations, petitioned European colonial powers to deny Italy loans and weapons, held prayer meetings, staged violent protests against colonial governments, and sought to join the Ethiopian military efforts against the Italian invaders.[55] However, despite the groundswell of popular support these mobilization efforts received from countless African communities around the world, African peoples were still, essentially, unorganized along any Pan-African lines. As a result, they lacked any significant amount of power to save Ethiopia from the ravages of Italian imperialism.

Post-WWII trends

The end of WWII, a decade after the Italian invasion of Ethiopia, meant the beginning of the end of colonialism proper in Africa. Factors associated with this development had a profound impact on the Pan-African movement. Like the Italian invasion earlier, experiences related to the end of WWII triggered the growth and development of Pan-African thought and action; they also contributed to the movement's further radicalization. One of the most stimulating factors during this period was the international espousal of the right of all people to independence and self-determination, contained in the Atlantic Charter. In response to Adolph Hitler's effort to colonize Europe, this document was created by the United States and Great Britain to galvanize global support to the Allied cause and to set the tone for post-WWII geopolitical rearrangements. No less significant was the fact that, once again, hundreds of thousands of African troops from the United States and the colonial dependencies in Africa and the Caribbean fought and died in this war—a war that was being touted as a war to defend the democratic ideals extolled in the Atlantic Charter. The effect of this experience on the African World was predictable: the willingness to tolerate racial inequality and national oppression plummeted to an all-time low. However, conditions were different from the previous World War. During the post-WWII period the imperialist powers would not succeed in denying, at least in principle, the right of African people on the continent, and soon afterwards in the Caribbean, to govern themselves. After the wreckage of WWII, the weakened European victors were in no position to reverse the anti-colonial movement that was gaining strength. This was especially true in light of the growing socialist threat in parts of Asia and Eastern Europe. And so it was in the context of these opportunities that the Pan-African movement, during and after WWII, became stronger and more militant.[56]

This development culminated to a large extent in the Fifth Pan-Africanist Congress of 1945 in Manchester, England. Organized by George Padmore, Kwame Nkrumah, and other important figures associated with the Pan-African Federation in Great Britain, this Congress symbolized, in many ways, the coming-of-age of Pan-Africanism.[57] It differed significantly from previous Pan-African meetings, conventions, and congresses in that: (1) the numerical participation of native-born Africans was greater; (2) there was a greater ratio of delegates who represented the organized labour of African workers and farmers; (3) the socialist world view clearly dominated in the discussions on the solution to the problems facing Africa and its scattered people; (4) the more passive and reformist resolutions passed in previous Pan-African meetings were replaced with more radical resolutions (one of which, written by Du Bois, did not rule out the use of force to achieve national liberation); and (5) a strategy to liberate Africa, *in Africa*, became the primary focus for the new, revolutionary Pan-Africanist agenda.

In less than two years, one of the direct outcomes of this congress began playing out in the erstwhile Gold Coast. From 1947 until Ghanaian independence in 1957, Nkrumah led his countrymen in a Positive Action campaign of mass strikes, boycotts, and demonstrations against British colonial rule. This strategy used by Nkrumah, blueprinted at the Manchester Congress, left the British with no other choice than to relinquish political power. The implications of this event for the rest of Africa and the entire African World were exceptional. With practically all of Global Africa, at that time, experiencing, in one form or another, political subjugation at the hands of powerful white nations, Ghana's independence in 1957 was hugely significant: it symbolized, at least in the hearts and minds of countless African descendants around the world, the beginning of a 'New World Order.' Fully grasping the huge historical moment of March 6, 1957, Nkrumah made his famous Pan-African declaration shortly after Ghana's *Garveyesque* flag rose to replace the descending British Union Jack. 'The Independence of Ghana is meaningless,' he roared, 'unless it's linked up with the total liberation of the African continent.'

It was at this juncture in the historical evolution of Pan-Africanism that Nkrumah became the leading ideological embodiment of the movement. Having absorbed all that came before him and all that surrounded him, Nkrumah, in 1957, wasted no time in building Ghana into what Malcolm X described as the 'Fountainhead of Pan-Africanism.'[58] In 1958, with the critical assistance of George Padmore, who Nkrumah appointed as his African Affairs Advisor, two conferences were convened in Accra that were historical milestones in the struggle for Pan-Africanism. The first one, held in April, was the Conference of Independent African States. The second, held in December of that same year, was the All-African Peoples Conference. While there were many important resolutions passed at these conferences, their real significance lay in the following: African leaders were meeting on African soil, for the first time, with the sole purpose of devising plans to liberate the entire African continent. In short, the mainspring of Pan-Africanism had returned home where it belonged.

These conferences, attended by Africans throughout the continent and abroad,[59] inspired the convening of other similar conferences held in Tunis in 1960, in Cairo in 1961, and in Ghana, again, in subsequent years. Other militant Pan-African formations and associations were now being created in abundance. One of the most important ones culminated in the Union of African States, first comprised of Ghana and Guinea in 1958, and later enlarged with the membership of Mali in 1960. Another significant formation occurred in 1959 during the Apartheid era in South Africa. A split in the African National Congress led to the creation of the Pan-Africanist Congress (PAC)—an organization of mostly youth who were heavily influenced by the radical ideas of South African nationalist, Anton Muziwakhe Lembede, and the Pan-Africanist writings of Du Bois, Garvey, Padmore, and Nkrumah. Led by Pan-Africanist Mangaliso Robert Sobukwe, PAC was guided by three main objectives: nationalism, socialism, and continental African unity.[60]

However, as more countries in Africa gained their independence, with as many as 17 having done so in 1960, a wide ideological rift began to grow. This rift, based squarely along class lines, coincided with the arrival of neo-colonialism on the African post-colonial scene.[61] With the critical assistance of an indigenous class of African facilitators, nay, puppets, the industrialized capitalist countries managed to ensure that, even with the advent of African political independence, economically things would remain the same. Africa's raw materials and mineral resources would continue to find their way, unhindered and unprocessed, to the factories and plants owned, in shares, by the banking and corporate interests of a collective imperialism located primarily in the United States, Western Europe, and Japan.

Among radical Pan-Africanists this was no secret. Frantz Fanon wrote passionately about it in the early 1960s, condemning the African petty bourgeoisie for serving as 'the transmission line between the nation and a capitalism, rampant though camouflaged, which today puts on the mask of neo-colonialism.'[62] And so it was in this context that a number of radical African countries, determined to unite Africa, outright, formed an association to pursue a genuine Union of African States. This group was called the Casablanca Group (so named after a conference they held in Morocco in January 1961). It consisted of Ghana, Guinea, Mali, Egypt, Algeria, Libya, and Morocco. In opposition to this Pan-African momentum, the Monrovia Group was formed in May 1961 to undermine the Casablanca Group's strength and potential outcome. This latter group was comprised of Liberia, Somalia, Nigeria, Sierra Leone, Congo-Brazzaville, Tunisia, Ethiopia, and several of the former French colonies, viz., La Cote d'Ivoire, Gabon, Chad, Senegal, Madagascar, and Cameroon. While forced to give lip service to the increasing demands for African unification, the countries comprising the Monrovia Group promoted a slow, gradualist approach, favouring regionalism over continental unification.

Out of this conflict between radical and liberal post-colonial forces in Africa emerged the compromised and deeply flawed Organization of African Unity (OAU), a loose association of countries that was incapable, even constitutionally, of meeting the radical demands of Pan-Africanism. Formed in May 1963, in Addis Ababa, the OAU limped along for approximately 40 years—underfunded and without any genuine authority or control over its member states. Its contributions (towards conflict management, economic cooperation, and the dismantling of colonialism) were so minor that they hardly warrant mentioning. Instead, it served as a major tool of neo-colonial control to help frustrate, rather than facilitate, the building of a united, socialist Africa.[63]

As the leader of radical Pan-Africanism, Nkrumah remained undeterred by the neo-colonial machinations that were engulfing him and his radical counterparts in other parts of Africa. Ghana under Nkrumah became a citadel of Pan-African synergy: a wide variety of organizational activities took place to enhance every shade and every phase of the Pan-African movement. This included the provision of all sorts of training and assistance to African freedom fighters from around the continent who were nestled in Ghana. It also resulted in the emergence, in Ghana, of a vibrant community of African Diasporans—activists, scholars, artists, and professionals, all of whom answered Nkrumah's call to return home and help build mother Africa.[64] Needless to say, imperialist forces, especially those sitting in London and Washington, DC, were not happy. And perhaps nothing earned their collective chagrin more than the 1965 publication of Nkrumah's *Neo-Colonialism: The Last Stage of Imperialism*. US President Lyndon B. Johnson had cause to be particularly peeved—*and he was*—if even a cursory reading of the chapter titled 'Monopoly Capitalism and the American Dollar' was made.[65] With the power of hindsight, then, the February 24, 1966 CIA inspired, funded, and orchestrated *coup d'état* that removed Nkrumah from Ghana seems almost natural.[66] Indeed,

the decade-long assault on Nkrumah and his government, both internally and externally, was relentless—ideologically, economically, and
militarily.[67]

With Malcolm X having been assassinated nearly one year earlier,
on February 21, 1965, the 1966 coup in Ghana was another major setback to the Pan-African movement. However, the emergence of the
Black Power movement that same year in the United States, and later
in other parts of the African World, represented the continuation and
spread of the Pan-African idea. Personified best by Trinidadian-born
Kwame Ture (formerly Stokely Carmichael), this radical movement was
strongly influenced by nationalist uprisings in Africa; it was also heavily
influenced by the work of Nkrumah, Sékou Touré, Frantz Fanon,
Julius Nyerere, and Malcolm X (whose courageous efforts, especially
during his post-Nation of Islam period, played a tremendous role in
shaping the consciousness of young activists towards Pan-Africanist
convictions). After exhausting all reformist means possible to end the
social degradation, economic exploitation, and political domination
that Africans in the United States were experiencing, a large sector of
young black activists in the Civil Rights Movement began seeing their
plight as indistinguishable from other African peoples in the Caribbean,
Europe, and Africa. As Nkrumah and Malcolm had encouraged, these
Black Power activists, as early 1968, began advocating that all peoples
of African descent were African, and that Pan-Africanism was the solution to the problems facing the entire African World.[68]

The regenerative effect of the Black Power movement continued
unabated with several Pan-African formations being established
during the early 1970s. The US-based African Liberation Support
Committee was one important formation during this time. One of its
main achievements was the contributions it made, early on, to African
Liberation Day celebrations in the United States during the early
1970s. The Black Consciousness Movement in South Africa, led by the
police-murdered Stephen Biko, was another huge development that was
influenced, significantly, by the Black Power movement. H. Rap Brown's
political biography, *Die Nigger Die*, for instance, was one of the many
writings of Black Power advocates that their counterparts in South
Africa were reading. The planning and convening of the Sixth Pan-
Africanist Congress (PAC), held in Tanzania in 1974, grew out of this
same energy. Although it failed to meet the expectations of many, the
Sixth PAC went far in reinforcing the primacy of class struggle within
the Pan-African movement. It also gave a powerful voice to the liberation struggles that were still being waged, mainly in Southern Africa.
These were no mean achievements.

However, the most significant activity during this period was the founding of the All-African People's Revolutionary Party (A-APRP) in 1972, shortly after Nkrumah's death. The A-APRP was created by African militants from different parts of the world, including Black Power activist Kwame Ture in the United States and Nkrumah protégé Lamin Jangha of the Gambia, both of whom worked with and studied under Nkrumah, as did Amilcar Cabral of Guinea Bissau, during Nkrumah's CIA-imposed sojourn in Guinea. Ture, Jangha, and others were committed to practicing the radical Pan-Africanist ideas espoused by Nkrumah, that is, Nkrumaism. Indeed, by 1972, the year of Nkrumah's passing, Nkrumaism—as outlined in the large number of books written and speeches made by Nkrumah—had congealed, nay, effloresced into an assimilation, derivation, synthesis, and refinement of the ideas espoused by Pan-African thinkers who preceded Nkrumah. Blyden, Hayford, Garvey, Du Bois, and Padmore are just some of the names that could be mentioned in this regard.[69] In short, Nkrumah's period in Guinea, under the shelter of Sékou Touré and the Democratic Party of Guinea, was an especially productive one for him and the Pan-African movement at-large: during this time, when the seeds of the A-APRP were first planted, he completed a number of critical works which, in conjunction with his earlier writings, provided the Pan-African movement with an urgently needed and finely tuned ideological compass.

During the 1980s, several events, some of them tragic, had a significant impact on the Pan-African movement. Sékou Touré's sudden death in 1984, and the subsequent right-wing coup in Guinea, created a significant loss to the movement because of the late president's dedication to the Pan-African cause. Other similar and decisive events that damaged the Pan-African movement during this period—devised by powerful western imperialist interests—include the assassinations of presidents Maurice Bishop of Grenada in 1983 and Thomas Sankara of Burkina Faso in 1987. In all three cases, because their revolutionary movements were completely dismantled, their deaths served to deprive the Pan-African movement of badly needed land bases—or what Nkrumah called 'Liberated Zones'—upon which further Pan-African activity could be better coordinated, consolidated, and enhanced.[70]

These 1980-setbacks were met with the demise of the Soviet Union in 1991, coupled with the fall of socialism in Eastern Europe (both of which affected, deeply, the international socialist movement). Despite these unfavourable conditions, the drive towards the realization of Pan-African objectives did not diminish during the last decade of the twentieth century. Instead, by the early 1990s, the deleterious effects neo-colonialism was having on African nation-states were so apparent, causing so much misery and grief (especially under the burden of IMF/ World Bank imposed conditionalities), that Pan-African thinkers and activists were left with no other choice besides intensifying their efforts against the common foe. One such effort involved the late Jamaican Pan-Africanist Dudley Thompson, who led a distinguished panel of Pan-Africanist leaders in holding the First Pan-African Conference on Reparations in Abuja, Nigeria, in April 1993. This conference represented a genuine milestone for the Pan-African movement. For the first time, ever, the movement for reparations was conjoined, fundamentally, with the movement to unite Global Africa. The proclamations made within the Abuja Declaration of 1993 were profound,[71] some of which are worth reproducing, at length, below:

> Convinced that the issue of reparations is an important question requiring the united action of Africa and its Diaspora and worthy of the active support of the rest of the international community,
>
> Fully persuaded that the damage sustained by the African people is not a 'thing of the past' but is painfully manifest in the damaged lives of contemporary Africans from Harlem to Harare, in the damaged economies of the black world from Guinea to Guyana, from Somalia to Surinam,
>
> Calls upon the international community to recognize that there is a unique and unprecedented moral debt owed to the African peoples which has Yet to be paid – the debt of compensation to the Africans as the most humiliated and exploited people of the last four centuries of modern history.

At this same conference, a proclamation for granting 'Right of Return' privileges to Africans in the Diaspora seeking repatriation was also made. Although it fell shy of providing citizenship for those seeking to return home, it did represent a very important first step in the process of 'Reuniting the African family.'

On the heels of this conference was the convening of the Seventh PAC a year later, held in Kampala, Uganda, in April 1994.[72] Like the Congress that preceded it, the Seventh PAC bled with contradictions and controversy. Nevertheless, it represented the largest gathering of participants in the history of the congresses: over 2,000 attended, a significant portion of whom represented grassroots organizations. Moreover, despite its vast shortcomings, at least three developments emerged out of this congress that have proven very helpful: (1) it raised the level of consciousness around the question of the liberation of African women to an all-time high; (2) it created a (long overdue) permanent PAC Secretariat, temporarily hosted by the Ugandan government; and (3) it brought to the fore the hotly debated and deeply divided topic of African Identity, that is, 'who is an African?,' particularly as it relates to those of Arab decent residing in North Africa.[73]

However, the Seventh PAC, as with all previous Pan-Africanist Congresses, save the fifth, did not have any significant impact on the mammoth task of politically educating and organizing the masses of African workers, famers, women, and students around the Pan-African cause. Indeed, this continued to be one of the main flaws of the Pan-Africanist Congresses. This was also symptomatic of the various other Pan-African meetings, conferences, and symposia that were held throughout much of the twentieth century. They usually talked the talk, but rarely walked the walk! In short, they went far in passing brilliant resolutions and making powerful declarations; however, they fell short in following up with the practical implementation of any of them. Instead, this laborious work was left in the hands of Pan-African activists who, through sheer dedication, have been engaged in this effort from times immemorial.

In the 1990s, the lion's share of this work fell into the hands of organizations like the Patrice Lumumba Coalition, the African People's Socialist Party, the Movement for Justice in Africa, the Pan-African Revolutionary Socialist Party, the Azania People's Organization, the A-APRP, and a legion of other local and international-based Pan-African organizations, most of which were founded in the 1970s. However, it was the A-APRP which had the greatest success during this period in establishing a presence in different parts of the African World, including the United States, Western Europe, (Western, Eastern, and Southern) Africa, and the Caribbean. Its leading spokesperson, the charismatic Kwame Ture, was dispatched, continuously, to different parts of the world to speak and to help organize chapters of the organization in various locales around the world. He achieved considerable success and was responsible, perhaps more than anyone else during this period, in keeping radical Pan-Africanism alive; he was especially effective among student populations on college campuses around the world. Sadly, in 1996 Ture was diagnosed with prostate cancer. However, for the two remaining years of life that he had left, though hobbled with the advanced stages of this deadly disease, Ture remained the unparalleled proponent of Nkrumaism in the world.

The new millennium

As the Pan-African movement rolled into the new millennium, perhaps its most defining experience, to date, has been the assassination of Colonel Muammar Qadhafi in October 2011. Its destructive aftermath was catastrophic: Africa's last remaining 'Liberated Zone,' the Great Socialist People's Libyan Arab Jamahiriya, was completely demolished. With the critical assistance of US predator drones, *remote-controlled from Las Vegas, Nevada (USA)*, and French fighter jets, NATO, forces carried it out. And they did so for one reason: to prevent the realization of Qadhafi's Pan-African ambitions for Africa. Indeed, Colonel Qadhafi was a Pan-Africanist *par excellence*. From his base in Libya, where his socialist policies produced the highest standard of living in Africa, he spent the first decade of the new millennium promoting African unity at a pace and level of militancy reminiscent of Nkrumah's vision and energy. He single-handedly drove African heads of state to replace the former OAU with the African Union (AU) in May 2001[74]; this was a laudable move by all accounts, despite the glaring deficiencies of the AU, given the OAU's dismal record of achievements. Speaking to a huge crowd in Accra in July 2000, en route to the very OAU meeting in Togo where he made his case for total continental unification, Qadhafi made this fundamental (Pan-African) point:

> The African people are one, the African continent is one; so is the African culture, as well as the miserable state in which all Africa was left by colonialism. We should not be deceived by anyone that there are differences inside Africa.[75]

And, like Nkrumah, he 'put his money where his mouth was!' The $300 million that Libya contributed towards the purchase of the continent's first communications satellite was groundbreaking: it enhanced, exponentially, the quality of communication for the entire continent.[76] This Libyan donation was out of a total cost of $377 million, and served to replace the $500 million annual leasing fee that Africa was paying Europe for the use of its satellites. It also provided the amount that, for years, the IMF, World Bank, the United States and Europe refused, despite promises, to provide for this same purpose.

Additionally, during this same decade, Colonel Qadhafi made a gallant effort to create a single African currency based on African gold deposits. Had this effort succeeded, his *Gold Dinar*, as a new revolutionary medium of exchange, would have caused giant repercussions to the dollar, pound, and franc that financiers in the United States, UK, and France would have found very difficult to repair. More importantly, the impact this single African currency would have had towards fostering greater African integration could have been, potentially, staggering. In fact, this quintessential Pan-African endeavour, alone, may have sealed his fate more than anything else. Even his efforts to block the advance of US AFRICOM manoeuvres throughout the continent—another one of his courageous, yet unsung, pursuits—probably pales in comparison. In short, the brutal murder of Colonel Muammar Qadhafi in October 2011, after decades of his Pan-African militancy in Africa and the world, was one of the worst blows the Pan-African movement has ever sustained.

Despite this momentous setback, the flame that has driven the Pan-African movement from times immemorial continues to burn in the new millennium. Shortly after the birth of the AU, and in response to its appeal to the African Diaspora to help in rebuilding Africa, the World African Diaspora Union (WADU) was created in 2004. Its mission, as envisioned by the late Pan-Africanist grassroots organizer, Elombe Brath, is consistent with the very core of Pan-Africanism itself: 'The Liberation, Unification, and Empowerment of African People, with One Central Government in Africa.'[77] And since its inception, WADU has organized various programmes and projects that have only served to enhance the Pan-Africanist cause. Fortunately, there remains, today, a large array of grassroots organizations in practically every corner of the African World designed, specifically, to meet the goals of Pan-Africanism.

However, the challenges facing the Pan-African movement remain as formidable as ever. The manipulation and intransigence of imperialist domination, especially in its late, aggressive neo-colonialist phase, is not the least of them. Indeed, the intent of the US AFRICOM menace, along with the multiplication of US drone bases dotting various regions of the continent, is crystal clear: to ensure the continued control, via the re-emergence of US 'Gunboat Diplomacy,' of Africa's mineral wealth. In this effort they are joined by various other predator nations with identical intentions. Nonetheless, the Pan-African movement's greatest challenge remains what has been plaguing it for centuries: the failure of Pan-African organizations to create, transnationally, a principled and disciplined unity to ensure common action in the pursuit of common goals and objectives. In short, the Pan-African movement has, for too long, been poorly coordinated with no umbrella organization designed to unite the various (genuinely) Pan-African organizations in their common struggle towards Pan-Africanism. This, more than anything else, explains why so many Pan-African organizations have been created over the years, only to soon be disbanded or to find themselves too weak and ineffective to make much of a difference in people's lives. Hence, while the motive driving the Pan-African movement remains as powerful as ever, the movement's growth, development, and ultimate success lie in what Nkrumah called for years ago: the formation of an institutional mechanism, a Pan-African party, designed to link Pan-African organizations under a common ideology in the pursuit of the common objective: one, united, socialist Africa.[78]

Notes

1 Malcolm X, *Malcolm X Speaks*, New York: Grove Press, 1965, pgs. 65,69.
2 Kwame Nkrumah, *Consciencism: Philosophy and Ideology for Decolonization*, New York: Monthly Review, 1964, pg. 72.
3 Marcus Garvey, Editorial in the *Negro World*, February 2, 1921. Quoted in 'An Apostle of Revolutionary Pan-Africanism' by Elombe Brath. *Caribbean Perspective*, Vol. 1, No. 3, pgs. 25–28.
4 Marcus Garvey, *The Philosophy and Opinions of Marcus Garvey or Africa for the Africans*, London: Frank Cass (Compiled by Amy Jacques Garvey), 1967, pgs. 52–53.
5 Colin Grant, *Negro with a Hat: The Rise and Fall of Marcus Garvey*, London: Vintage Books, 2009, pgs. 184–435.
6 Kwame Nkrumah, *Handbook of Revolutionary Warfare: A Guide to the Armed Phase of the African Revolution*, New York: International, 1968, pg. 28.
7 W.E.B. Du Bois, *The World and Africa: An Enquiry into the Part Which Africa Has Played in World Affairs*, New York: International, 1965, pg. 310. This socialist prescription was merely an extension of ones made, decades earlier, at the Pan-Africanist Congresses held in Europe during the first quarter of the twentieth century. Indeed, as early as 1923, at the Third Pan-Africanist Congress, one of the main resolutions demanded, 'The organization of commerce and industry so as to make the main objects of capital and labour the welfare of the many rather than the enriching of the few,' George Padmore, *Pan-Africanism or Communism?* New York: Doubleday, 1972, pg. 118.
8 See the mammoth study by Imanuel Geiss, *The Pan-African Movement: A History of Pan-Africanism in America, Europe, and Africa*, New York: Africana Publishing, 1974, pgs. x–iv, 3–40, for a typical Eurocentric account of the origins of Pan-Africanism.
9 Ibid., pgs. 174–282.
10 Colin Grant, *Negro with a Hat*, op cit., pgs. 160–297.
11 Owen Charles Mathurin, *Henry Sylvester Williams and the Origin of the Pan-African Movement, 1869–1911*, Wesport, CT: Greenwood Press, 1976.

12 James T. Campbell, *Middle Passages: African American Journeys to Africa, 1787–2005*, London: Penguin, 2006, pgs. 15–56.

13 Ibid., pgs. 15–135.

14 Molefi Kete Asante, *The History of Africa: The Quest for Eternal Harmony*, New York: Routledge, 2007, pgs. 183–201.

15 Chancellor Williams, *Destruction of Black Civilization: Great Issues of a Race from 4500 to 2000 A.D.*, Chicago: Third World Press, 1992.

16 Cheik Anta Diop, *The Cultural Unity of Black Africa: The Domains of Patriarchy and of Matriarchy in Classical Antiquity*, London: Karnak House, 1989.

17 Tony Martin, *The Pan-African Connection: From Slavery to Garvey and Beyond*, Dover, MA: The Majority Press, 1983, pgs. 4–5.

18 James T. Campbell, *Middle Passages*, op cit., pgs. 15–56; Christopher Clapham, *Liberia and Sierra Leone: An Essay in Comparative Politics*, London: Cambridge, pg. 5; George Padmore, *Pan-Africanism or Communism?*, op cit., 1972, pgs. 1–53.

19 Arna Bontemps and Jack Conroy, *Any Place But Here*, New York: Hill & Wang, 1966; Syed Anwar Hossain, *Back to Africa Movement*, Dhaka, Bangladesh: Dana Prokashoni, 1983; Floyd Miller, *The Search for a Black Nationality: Black Emigration and Colonization, 1787–1863*, Chicago: University of Illinois, 1975.

20 Henry Highland Garnet, 'Henry Highland Garnet's Speech at an Enthusiastic Meeting of the Colored Citizens of Boston,' in Sterling Stuckey, *Ideological Origins of Black Nationalism*, Boston: Beacon, 1972, pg. 183.

21 Tony Martin, 'Some Reflections on Evangelical Pan-Africanism or Black Missionaries and the Struggle for African Souls, 1890–1930,' in *The Pan-African Connection*, op cit., pgs. 31–46; Sylvia M. Jacobs, ed., *Black Americans and the Missionary Movement in Africa*,' Westport, CT: Praeger, 1982; Sylvia M. Jacobs, 'Say Africa When You Pray: The Activities of Early Black Baptist Women Missionaries Among Liberian Women and Children,' *SAGE* 3 (Fall, 1986), pgs. 16–21.

22 Colin Grant, *Negro with a Hat*, op cit., pgs. 168–169; Thomas Henriksen, 'African Intellectual Influences on Black Americans: The Role of Edward W. Blyden,' *Phylon* 36 (September, 1975), pgs. 279–290; Hollis R. Lynch, *Edward Blyden: Pan-Negro Patriot, 1832–1912*, London: Oxford University, 1967.

23 William E. Phipps, *William Sheppard: Congo's African-American Livingstone*, Louisville, KY: Geneva Press, 2002; Pagan Kennedy, *Black Livingston: A True Tale of Adventure in the Nineteenth-Century Congo*, New York: Viking, 2002.

24 John Hope Franklin, 'George Washington Williams and Africa' in *Africa and the Afro-American Experience: Eight Essays*. (Lorraine A. Williams, Ed.), Washington, DC: Howard University Press, 1977, pg. 65.

25 Jean-Germain Gros, '"Unknown Soldiers": Forgotten Haitian Pan-Africanists from the Distant and Recent Past,' *Nkrumaist Review: Pan-African Perspectives on African Affairs*, Vol. 4, No. 1, June 2008, pgs. 2–9.
26 Ibid., pg. 3.
27 Tony Martin, 'Benito Sylvain of Haiti on the Pan-African Conference of 1900,' in *The Pan-African Connection*, op cit, pgs. 201–216.
28 Marco Aurelio Schaumloeffel, *Tabom: The Afro-Brazilian Community in Ghana*, CreateSpace, 2008; Kwame Essien, ' "Afie Ni Afie" (Home is Home): Revisiting Reverse Trans-Atlantic Journeys to Ghana and the Paradox of Return,' *A Journal of African Migration*, www.africamigration.com/Issue%207/Articles/HTML/essien_home_is_home.htm
29 For example, 206 men, women, and children who boarded the ship, Azor, in the spring of 1878, en route to Liberia, were seen off by a throng of 10,000 well-wishers at the harbor in Charleston, South Carolina. See James T. Campbell, *Middle Passages*, op cit., pgs. 110–111.
30 Ayo J. Langley, 'Chief Sam's African Movement and Race Consciousness in West Africa,' *Phylon* 32 (1971), pgs. 164–178; Robert A. Hill, 'Before Garvey: Chief Alfred Sam and the African Movement, 1912–1916,' in *Pan-African Biography*, edited by Robert A. Hill, Los Angeles: African Studies Center, 1987; William E. Bittle and Gilbert Geis, *The Longest Way Home: Chief Alfred C. Sam's Back-to-Africa Movement*, Detroit: Wayne State, 1964.
31 P. Olisanwuche Esedebe, *Pan-Africanism: The Idea and the Movement, 1776–1963*, Washington, DC: Howard University, 1982, pgs. 23–25.
32 Edwin W. Smith, *The Christian Mission in Africa: A Study Based on the Work of the International Conference at Le Zoute, Belgium: September 14th to 21st, 1926*, London: International Missionary Council, 1926, pgs. 122–124.
33 See Michael Williams, *Pan-Africanism: An Annotated Bibliography*, Pasadena, CA: Salem Press, 1992, pgs. 34–40, for a wide range of books and articles on this topic.
34 W.E.B Du Bois, 'Africa and the American Negro Intelligentsia,' *Apropos of Africa: Afro-American Leaders and the Romance of Africa* (Adelaide Cromwell Hill and Martin Kilson, eds.), 1956, New York: Doubleday, p. 374.
35 Casely Hayford, inspired earlier by Blyden, communicated with Du Bois and Garvey during this period, and wrote one of the most important books on Pan-Africanism a decade earlier: *Ethiopia Unbound: Studies on Race Emancipation*, 1911; see also, Immanuel Geiss, *The Pan-African Movement*, op cit., pgs. 284–293.
36 G.I.C. Eluwa, 'Background to the Emergence of the National Congress of British West Africa,' *African Studies Review*, 1971, Vol. 14, No. 2, pgs. 205–218.
37 Keni Mbingu, 'A State of Siege: Repression and Cultural Emasculation in Kenya,' *Philosophy and Social Action*, 17 (3–4), July–December, 1991, pgs. 9–17; Emmy Godwin Irobi, 'Ethnic Conflict Management in

Africa: A Comparative Case Study of Nigeria and South Africa,' 2005: www. beyondintractability.org/casestudy/irobi-ethnic; Douglass Little, 'Cold War and Colonialism in Africa: The United States, France, and the Madagascar Revolt 1947,' *Pacific Historical Review*, Vol. 59, No. 4, November 1990.

38 John McCracken, *A History of Malawi, 1859–1966*. Woodbridge: James Currey, 2012; Joey Power, *Political Culture and Nationalism in Malawi: Building Kwacha*, New York: University of Rochester Press, 2010.

39 See Colin Grant, *Negro with a Hat*, op cit., London: Vintage, 2008 for a detailed account of the role of the US federal government, under the supervision of J. Edgar Hoover, in derailing the Garvey movement.

40 Tony Martin, *The Pan-African Connections*, op cit., pg. 19.

41 The large volume of work of Tony Martin remains one of the most invaluable sources of information on Garvey and the UNIA. See also Colin Grant, *Negro with a Hat*, op cit., John Henrik Carke (with Amy Jacques Garvey), *Marcus Garvey and the Vision of Africa*, New York: Vintage Books, 1974, and *The Marcus Garvey and Universal Negro Improvement Association Papers*, Vols. I–XI, Robert A. Hill, ed.

42 See Colin Grant, *Negro with A Hat*, op cit., pgs. 168–169.

43 Marcus Garvey, *Blackman*, December 30, 1939.

44 For a summary of the some of the contributions African women have made to the Pan-African movement, see Michael Williams, 'Unsung Heroines of Pan-Africanism: A Preliminary Assessment,' *Abafazi: The Simmons College Review of Women of African Descent*, Vol. 3, No. 1, Fall 1992, pgs. 3–9. See, also, Barbara Ransby, *Eslanda: The Large and Unconventional Life of Mrs. Paul Robeson*, New Haven, CT: Yale University Press, 2013; Gerald Horne, *Race Woman: The Lives of Shirley Graham Du Bois*, New York: NYU Press, 2000; and Tony Martin, *Amy Ashwood Garvey, Pan-Africanist, Feminist and Mrs. Marcus Garvey No. 1, Or, A Tale of Two Amies*, Dover, MA: Majority Press, 2007 for three excellent studies on three of the most important female Pan-Africanists of the twentieth century.

45 Tony Martin, *Amy Ashwood Garvey*, op cit.

46 See Amy Jacques Garvey, *Garvey and Garveyism*, New York: Collier-MacMillan, 1970. Amy Jacques also compiled the very influential, *Philosophy and Opinions of Marcus Garvey or Africa for the Africans*, London: Frank Cass, 1967 (to raise funds while her husband was in prison awaiting trial), and co-edited with E.U. Essien-Udom, *More Philosophy and Opinions of Marcus Garvey*, London: Frank Cass, 1977.

47 Colin Grant, *Negro with a Hat*, op cit., pgs. 166–168, 384–385.

48 Olisanwuche P. Esedebe, *Pan-Africanism*, op cit., pgs. 79–110.

49 Tony Martin, *Amy Ashwood Garvey*, op cit., pg. 86.

50 Colin Grant, *Negro with a Hat*, op cit., pgs. 176–183.

51 Immanuel Geiss, *The Pan-African Movement*, op cit., 297–304; Olisanwuche Esedebe, *Pan-Africanism*, op cit., pgs. 79–110; C.L.R. James, *Nkrumah and the Ghana Revolution*, Westport, CT: Lawrence Hill, pg. 62.

52 P. Kiven Tunteng, 'Padmore's Impact on Africa: A Critical Appraisal,' *Phylon* 35 (March, 1974), pgs. 33–44.

53 C.L.R. James, 'Abyssinia and the Imperialist,' *The Keys* (January–March, 1936); also quoted in Olisanwuche Esedebe, *Pan-Africanism*, op cit., pg. 118.

54 The evolution of Pan-Africanism in Africa was not unaffected by the Italian invasion of Ethiopia. See S.S. Quarcoopome, 'The Politics and Nationalism of A.W. Kojo Thompson: 1924–1944,' *Research Review NS*, Vol. 7, Nos. 1 and 2, 1991, pg. 7.

55 Robert Weisbord, *Ebony Kinship: Africa, Africans, and the Afro-American*, Westport, CT: Greenwood, 1973, pgs. 89–114; James H. Meriwether, *Proudly We Can Be African: Black Americans and Africa: 1935–1961*, Chapel Hill: UNC Press, 2002.

56 J. Ayodele Langley, *Pan-Africanism and Nationalism in West Africa 1900–1945: A Study in Ideology and Social Classes*, London: Oxford University Press, 1973, pgs. 326–368; Penny M. Von Eschen, *Race Against Empire: Black Americans and Anti-Colonialism, 1937–1957*, Ithaca, NY: Cornell University Press, 1997.

57 George Padmore, *Pan-Africanism or Communism?* op cit., pgs. 130–161.

58 Malcolm X, *Malcolm X Speaks*, op cit., 1965, pg. 62.

59 Eslanda Goode Robeson, for example, attended the All-African Peoples Conference in December of 1958 and spoke at the conference on the need for greater female participation in the struggle. See 'The Accra Conference,' *New World Review*, February 1959; reprinted in 'Remembrances of Eslanda,' *Freedomways*, Vol. 6, No. 4, Fall, 1966, pg. 349.

60 Benjamin Pogrund, *Robert Sobukwe, How Can Man Die Better*, Johannesburg: Jonathan Ball Publishers, 1997; See Inaugural Speech Robert Sobukwe made in April 1959: www.sahistory.org.za/archive/robert-sobukwe-inaugural-speech-april-1959.

61 See Frantz Fanon, *The Wretched of the Earth*, New York: Grove, 1963.

62 Ibid., pg. 152.

63 Elenga M'Buyinga, *Pan-Africanism or Neo-Colonialism: The Bankruptcy of the O.A.U.*, London: Zed, 1982.

64 Tom Feelings, *The Middle Passage: White Ships, Black Cargo*, New York: Dial Books, Preface; Kevin K. Gaines, *American Africans in Ghana: Black Expatriates and the Civil Rights Era*, Chapel Hill: UNC Press, 2006.

65 Kwame Nkrumah, *Neo-Colonialism: The Last Stage of Imperialism*, New York: International, 1965, pg. 52–68.

66 The role of the CIA in the overthrow of Kwame Nkrumah is uncontested and fully documented. The large volume of relevant declassified National Security Council and Central Intelligence Agency documents speaks for itself. See www.seeingblack.com/x060702/nkrumah.shtml (among a wide array of documentary evidence on line). See also, *The Great Deception: The Role of the CIA in the Overthrow of Nkrumah*, Accra: Socialist Forum of Ghana, 2012; See also: Charles Quist-Adade, 'How Did a Fateful CIA Coup—Executed 55 Years Ago This February 24—Doom Much of Sub-Saharan Africa?,' *CovertAction Magazine*, February 24, 2021, retrieved from: https://covertactionmagazine.com/2021/02/24/how-did-a-fateful-cia-coup-executed-55-years-ago-this-february-24-doom-much-of-sub-saharan-africa/.

67 Eboe Hutchful (ed.), *The IMF and Ghana: The Confidential Record*, London: Zed, 1988.

68 Stokely Carmichael, *Stokely Speaks: Black Power Back to Pan-Africanism*, New York: Vintage, 1981. See also, Malcolm X, *The Autobiography of Malcolm X*, New York: Grove, 1965, in which he described the contents of his private talk with Kwame Nkrumah while visiting Ghana in 1964: 'We discussed the unity of Africans and people of African descent. We agreed that Pan-Africanism was the key also to the problems of those of African heritage,' pg. 357.

69 Michael Williams, 'Marcus Garvey and Kwame Nkrumah: A Case of Ideological Assimilation, Advancement and Refinement,' *The Western Journal of Black Studies*, Vol. 7, No. 2, Summer 1983, pgs. 94–102; and 'Nkrumahism as an Ideological Embodiment of Leftist Thought Within the African World,' *Journal of Black Studies*, Vol. 15, No. 1, September 1984, pgs. 117–134.

70 Kwame Nkrumah, *Handbook*, op cit., New York: International, 1968, pgs. 43–50.

71 See 'Abuja Proclamation of 1993,' www.africanconstitution.org/home/abuja-proclamation.

72 'Rebuilding the Pan African Movement: A Report on the 7th Pan African Congress,' *African Journal of Political Science New Series*, Vol. 1, No. I, June 1996, Guest Editor's Introduction, pgs. 1–8.

73 See Chapter 4 for a discussion on this critical question.

74 The flaws and failings of the elite-driven AU are too numerous to discuss, at length, now, but will be taken up in subsequent chapters.

75 Muammar Qadhafi, 'Muammar Al Qathafi: Leader of the Great Al-Fateh Revolution and the Great Socialist Peoples Libyan Arab Jamahiriya Speaks to the People of Ghana, Accra, Ghana – 8th July 2000,' *Nkrumaist Review: Pan-African Perspectives on African Affairs*, Vol. 1, No. 2, December 2000, pgs. 21–24.

76 Jean-Paul Pougala, 'The Lies Behind the West's War on Libya,' *Libya 360*, 2011.

77 WADU website: www.wadupam.org/.

78 Kwame Nkrumah, *Handbook*, op cit., New York: International, 1968, pgs. 56–58.

2 Nkrumaism and radical Pan-African thought

Within Global Africa there has been a plethora of congruence in thought and action in the struggle against the particular forms of national oppression, class exploitation, and gender domination experienced by the African people. This has been the case from times immemorial. Indeed, the record is fairly clear that Africans on the mainland and those in the diaspora have been suffering from and responding to a common historical experience in a manner that has not been qualitatively different from one region of the world to another.[1] This congruence has been personified in the parallel movements and ideas associated with a legion of revolutionary nationalists and socialists within the African World. Despite this commonality, the Pan-African movement, in particular, has not been well anchored, ideologically. However, this dearth of ideological accord that has plagued the Pan-African movement should not be interpreted to mean that no such ideological system exists that is capable of galvanizing, harnessing, and amalgamating the energies of the Pan-African community into common action. As this study attempts to demonstrate, Nkrumaism, the consistent and coherent body of ideas, programmes, policies, and principles espoused and practiced by Osagyefo Dr. Kwame Nkrumah, is best suited to filling this void.

In fact, Nkrumaism, more than any other body of ideas, shares an organic link—as an ideological assimilation, advancement, and refinement—with progressive and radical ideas that emerged and developed within the Pan-African community before and during Nkrumah's lifetime. And to date, 50 years after his passing, the veracity of this contention remains intact. C.L.R. James recognized this reality years ago and noted the unique biographical experience Nkrumah underwent during his years abroad in the United States and London:

> Not only in books but in his contact with people and his very active intellectual and political life, he was the inheritor of the centuries of

DOI: 10.4324/9781003224990-3

material struggle and intellectual thought which the Negro people in the United States had developed from all sources in order to help them in their effort to emancipate themselves. Nkrumah had an astonishing capacity to learn, and there was much to learn in United States that has not yet found its place in books ... After this shaping experience, in London he found himself at the centre of the highly political consciousness of post-war Europe within which had grown ideas and organizations for years especially devoted to the cause which had always been the centre of his life.[2]

What Nkrumah was able to construct out of the Pan-African thought preceding and surrounding him—thought which reflected the actual suffering and concrete struggles experienced throughout Global Africa—is tantamount to what Karl Marx was able to fashion out of the thought of imminent European thinkers during the pre-advanced stage of industrial capitalism.[3] With Marx, theorists who readily come to mind include British political economists (e.g., Adam Smith, David Ricardo, and others), French utopian socialists (e.g., Henri de Saint-Simon, Charles Fourier, and others), and German classical philosophers (e.g., Immanuel Kant, Georg Wilhelm Friedrich Hegel, and others). In both cases, ideas were digested, assimilated, cultivated, jettisoned, refined, corrected, expanded, and advanced into a systematic new whole.

***

In this chapter, an effort will be made to demonstrate the contention above by comparing and contrasting Nkrumaism with a representative sample of some of the most radical and prominent ideas that have emerged from the Pan-African movement over the past two millennia. This sample would have to include, minimally, the thought of persons such as W.E.B. DuBois, Marcus Garvey, C.L.R. James, George Padmore, Amy Jacques Garvey, Sékou Touré, Frantz Fanon, Julius Nyerere, Malcolm X, and Kwame Ture (during the period when he served as the chief spokesperson for the Black Power movement).[4] In illustrating the parallels between Nkrumaism and the aforementioned sample of Pan-Africanist thinkers, such an examination would have to demonstrate which ideas are derived from, compatible with, and an advancement of ideas that are being suggested links Nkrumaism with this body of thought over the suggested time period. Needless to say, there are a number of great Pan-Africanist thinkers not included in this sample who could have easily been included. Nonetheless, the wide gamut of ideas that have emerged in the struggle to achieve Pan-Africanism is more likely than not covered in the pantheon listed earlier.

Analysis

Subsumed under the conceptual category of nationalism are several relevant units of analysis that can be used in this discussion, beginning with the concept of identity. Despite his tendency to vacillate on this question, Du Bois was lucid in one of his more seminal studies, *The Negro*, in defining the identity of even the so-called mulatto as African.[5] And even when using different concepts to describe Africans (such as coloured, Negro, Black, and others), he normally applied these concepts in their broadest (Pan-African) meaning. As far as Garvey was concerned, all people of African descent were the same and he saw 'absolutely no difference between the native African and the American and West Indian Negroes, in that we are descendants from one family stock.'[6] This classification was not compromised by Garvey, even in his confrontation with light-skinned Africans such as Du Bois.[7] In the case of Malcolm X, his conceptualization of the African identity went beyond just a racial classification; it also included the concept of culture as well.[8] And standing on the ideological edifice of Malcolm, while personifying, so well, the militant aspirations of the Black Power movement (which had a significant impact on Nkrumah), Kwame Ture, as early as 1968, began sharpening his analysis to include the concept of the African identity in his advocacy.[9] As is being contended, these conceptualizations of the African identity are completely incorporated into the ideological system of Nkrumaism, which holds as one of its basic principles: 'All peoples of African descent, whether they live in North or South America, the Caribbean, or in any other part of the world are Africans and belong to the African nation.'[10]

The critical role of Africa in the liberation of Global Africa has been given considerable attention by many Pan-Africanist thinkers as well. To a large extent, the numerous Pan-African conferences, congresses, and conventions organized during the first half of the twentieth century by Garvey, DuBois, and other Pan-Africanists are a clear expression of this. DuBois was very lucid on this point, stating that, 'until Africa is free, the descendants of Africa the world over cannot escape chains.'[11] Considered the 'Father of Pan-Africanism' by many, DuBois felt that Africans throughout the world should contribute to freeing Africa because, 'any ebullition of action and feeling that results in amelioration of the lot of Africa tends to ameliorate the conditions of colored people throughout the world.'[12] Garvey, perhaps more than anyone else before him, popularized the notion of the primacy of Africa in the struggle of Africans worldwide. He consistently challenged the African masses to 'build up in Africa a government of our own, big enough and strong enough to protect Africa and Negroes everywhere.'[13] According to Garvey, there was no other land base in the world that Africans had any other just claim to and that was more important than their own 'Mother Africa.'[14] Amy Jacques Garvey, Marcus Garvey's second wife, who carried the Pan-Africanist torch long after her husband's passing, wrote frequently and vociferously to her followers, once 'to remind those in alien lands that Africa is their ancestral home, and it is their duty, in common with those at home, to make of it an earthly paradise.'[15] Malcolm X was also very clear about the critical and primary role that the liberation of Africa will play in the liberation of Global Africa.[16] Malcolm consistently taught his listeners the importance of land, arguing that 'revolutions are fought to get control of land,' and that the African people, especially in the United States, were in such 'a very low condition' because they 'had no control whatsoever over any land.'[17] And as a rapidly developing Pan-Africanist, Malcolm felt strongly that 'the only hope for the black man in America [is] in a strong Africa.'[18] For this reason he warned Africans in the United States that any organization that was not based in Africa could not be effective.[19] As in the case with identity, the notion of the liberation of Africa as the primary precondition for the liberation of Africans, globally, is one of the cardinal principles of Nkrumaism: 'The total liberation and the unification of Africa under an All-African socialist government must be the primary objective of all Black revolutionaries throughout the world.'[20]

The idea of a united Africa has a conceptual history similar to other notions subsumed under this nationalist category. DuBois,[21] Garvey,[22] Touré,[23] Fanon,[24] and many other Pan-Africanist thinkers have contributed to its development. Before Nkrumah, however, George Padmore gave this idea its most precise meaning, including the strategy towards achieving it.[25] Nkrumaism has not only digested these ideas on African unity, but also provides a refinement of Padmore's thesis on this subject and an advancement of DuBois' notions as well. As a result of his experiences with the machinations of neo-colonialism, Nkrumah eliminated Padmore's regionalist stage towards African unity. He argued that 'the idea of regional federations in Africa [was] fraught with many dangers' because of the risk of regional loyalties developing in Africa favourable 'for foreign intervention, interferences and subversion' by the imperialist powers in their struggle to balkanize Africa.[26] With Du Bois, whereas his concept of a united Africa included, for the most part, only 'Black Africa,' 'from the Sahara to the Indian Ocean,'[27] Nkrumah's conceptualization included the entire African continent.[28]

This extension is an integral part of Nkrumah's philosophical notion of the need for Africa to embrace all of its past, including the traditional, the Arab-Islamic, and the Euro-Christian. Indeed, as Nkrumah warned years ago, it is critical that the latter two experiences, both important in Africa's evolution, be digested and assimilated into the tapestry of African cultural patterns in such a way as to ensure societal peace and harmony while elevating Africa's humanist and egalitarian past.[29] In this way, the African Personality becomes both inclusive and dynamic. This is significantly different from a simple appreciation of the cultural (and psychological) damage Africa has been subjected to over the centuries, which most Pan-Africanist thinkers, including Nkrumah, have acknowledged.[30] However, rather than arguing that Africans should simply reject this cultural imposition, as Garvey advocated,[31] and return to their traditional past, as Nyerere had encouraged,[32] Nkrumaism recognizes the 'Split Personality' that plagues African society and offers, as a solution, a synthesis of these three strands. This synthesis is incorporated in the Nkrumaist concept of Philosophical Consciencism, which provides an intellectual map to 'enable African society to digest the Western and Islamic and the Euro-Christian elements in Africa, and develop them in such a way that they fit into the African Personality.'[33]

Socialism, as a conceptual category, and several other closely related notions, can also be used to aid in the examination of this proposition. Socialism and the class struggle have been an integral part of the Pan-African movement since the first quarter of the twentieth century. They are, for this reason, an integral part of the ideological inheritance of which Nkrumaism is partially composed. However, it is worth noting that the socialist world view that influenced Nkrumah did so only after it entered the prism of the Pan-Africanist thought that surrounded him during the early period of his ideological development in the United States. As C.L.R. James reflected, Nkrumah was imbibed with 'the ideas of Marx, Lenin and other revolutionaries worked out chiefly by people of African descent in Western Europe, and America, to be used for the emancipation of the people of Africa.'[34]

Of the ten Pan-Africanist thinkers in this sample, Garvey, Nyerere, Malcolm, and Ture demonstrated the least clarity on the question of the class struggle as the primary vehicle to be used in the building of socialism in a united Africa. Garvey never formally espoused socialism, partially because of the ascendancy of race during his day, with Africans, globally, hardly divided along the rigid class lines that has become so prevalent since the beginning of the post-colonial period. Consequently, he often stated that 'you have no fight among yourselves between capital and labor, because all of us are labourers, therefore we need not be socialists.'[35] His feelings towards socialism were also conditioned by, and directed against, those persons and organizations that considered themselves the practitioners of this doctrine within the United States in their attempt to infiltrate the Garvey movement and destroy it.[36] However, Garvey never gave a blanket condemnation of socialism or communism, choosing instead to qualify his critique: 'I am advising the Negro working man and labourer against the present brand of communism or worker's Partisanship as taught in America.'[37] In gist, Garvey's disenchantment was not against socialism, per se, but against those persons and organizations who attempted to practice it, and who harboured chauvinistic attitudes on crucial questions and issues facing the African majority. Nevertheless, it is clear from analyzing Garvey's *Philosophy and Opinions* that he was staunchly opposed to any form of socio-economic distinctions among the African masses.[38] In fact, the only distinctions that Garvey foresaw in the new Africa he was struggling to build 'would be based upon service and loyalty to race.'[39] He was adamant on this point because of the centuries of oppression and exploitation Africans had suffered at the hands of Europeans. 'Therefore,' he argued, the African 'is not prepared to tolerate a similar assumption on the part of his own people.'[40] For these reasons, although Garvey's class analysis was weak, his penchant for brotherhood and equality are by no means contradictory to the Nkrumaist desire for socialism. In fact, they can be seen as contributing elements to the leftist germ that Nkrumah was influenced by and eventually developed further.

With Malcolm, while he believed, fervently, that a strong Africa is the African's only hope, wherever he or she is, he never really defined what he meant by a strong Africa, besides being united and independent. Even though Malcolm's full-scale entry into Pan-Africanism meant an accompanying and rapidly growing distaste for capitalism and attraction to socialism,[41] he never had the opportunity to develop such an analysis. However, Nkrumaism provides such an analysis, which includes Malcolm's specific fascination with what he called 'African Socialism,' that is, 'a form of socialism that fits into the African context.'[42] While exposing the neo-colonial underpinnings of the African bourgeoisie's fascination with *African Socialism*, Nkrumah defined scientific socialism in perfect consistency with what appealed to Malcolm, arguing that the particularity of its form does not deny the universality of its essence.[43]

On the notion of the class struggle, while Nyerere was opposed to capitalism and its many derivatives, and decided that socialism was the path of development the African Revolution should follow, his idealist approach to achieving socialism denied the objectivity of the class structures and divergent class interests that actually existed in Tanzania and the rest of Africa, and that the materialist analysis of Nkrumaism uncovers. Instead, all Nyerere concedes is that Africans have accepted a class or 'capitalist mentality.' Therefore, he rejected the class struggle and instead opted for a recapturing of the traditional African mentality as a solution to Africa's problems since, according to him, there were no classes in Africa before European colonialism and the advent of the 'capitalist mentality.'[44] For his part, Nyerere was wrong on both accounts: Africa prior to European colonialism was not devoid of class distinctions or class conflict;[45] and second, class cleavages and class exploitation exist in African society today, concretely, and not just in the mentality of some capitalist-minded Africans.[46] Nkrumaism captures this socio-economic reality, correcting the mistakes found in Nyerere's analysis due to his idealist approach and false assumption about Africa's pre-colonial history. With regard to Nyerere's romanticism with pre-colonial Africa, the Nkrumaist rebuttal is more consistent with the historical facts: 'Colonialism deserves to be blamed for many evils in Africa, but surely it was not preceded by an African Golden Age or Paradise.'[47] In short, there is 'no historical or even anthropological evidence' to support the contention that African society throughout the period before the European invasion was classless.[48]

As for the supposed absence of the class struggle in Africa today, Nkrumah demonstrated that theorists who made this mistake were diluted by the temporary national unity between all classes in Africa during the anti-colonial struggle. In gist, the class struggle was blurred for a while. However, Nkrumah explained that it was during the struggle to build socialism that the class cleavages, 'which had been temporarily submerged in the struggle to win political freedom,' reappeared.[49] The conflict between African workers, rural and urban, and the African bourgeoisie—the latter whose 'basic interest lies in preserving capitalist social and economic structures'—is the essential conflict in Africa today.'[50] This, according to Nkrumah, is only because the African bourgeoisie is 'in alliance with international monopoly finance capital and neocolonialism';[51] consequently, 'they provide the main means by which international monopoly finance continues to plunder Africa and to frustrate the purposes of the African Revolution.'[52] Nyerere's analysis failed to take into account these realities. For these reasons, the Nkrumaist analysis lays bare the obstacles that prevent Nyerere from reaching his socialist objectives, which are embodied in the class struggle.

While in Guinea during the late 1960s, Nkrumah dedicated special attention to correcting what he felt were some of the erroneous ideas that were produced by the Black Power movement that Kwame Ture and others of his generation were espousing; he felt these ideas were detrimental to the ideological development of Global Africa.[53] This task was set forth in Nkrumah's article 'The Spectre of Black Power,'[54] first published in 1968, and to some extent in *Class Struggle in Africa*.[55] The corrections centred around Ture's failure to grasp the significance of the class struggle relative to the struggle against racism and national oppression. The essence of the Nkrumaist position, which rejects the primacy of race over class as an explanatory variable in determining the fundamental and principal adversary of the African Revolution, is summed up as follows: 'Racial discrimination is the product of an environment, an environment of a divided class society, and its solution is to change that environment.'[56] Ture's understanding of the Pan-African movement during this time did not include an understanding of its relationship to the international socialist revolution. Instead, he understood it only in racial terms, as expressed in his open letter from Guinea read at the opening of Malcolm X Liberation University in October 1969. In this letter he stated: 'Right now we are in a cold war with America and Europe. When we begin to move militarily on all fronts, it will be an all-out race war, Africa versus Europe.'[57]

This is the reason Ture refused, for a while, to embrace socialism completely, on one occasion arguing: 'In their form neither communism nor socialism speak to the problem of racism.'[58] Nkrumah opposed this type of thinking adamantly, asserting that only 'the attainment of world communism can provide the condition under which the race question can finally be abolished and eliminated.'[59] Furthermore, Nkrumah felt it necessary to warn the African left in the United States 'to be on its guard against the internal as well as the external enemy' in response to Ture's inability to see the internal class enemies of the African Revolution.[60] In other words, Ture's contention that 'every Negro is a potential black man,'[61] and his willingness to work with bourgeois lawyers and politicians within the African community in the United States, even as late as 1970,[62] blinded him from seeing the veracity of the Nkrumaist revelation: 'It is the indigenous bourgeoisie who provide the main means by which international monopoly finance continues to … frustrate the purposes of the African Revolution.'[63]

This clear-cut class analysis of Nkrumaism is not without ideological precedence or congruence within the sample of Pan-African thinkers chosen for this study. DuBois, whose commitment to socialism can be traced back to as early as 1900, warned the new African heads of state that 'a body of local capitalists, even if they are black, can never free Africa; they will simply sell it into new slavery to old masters overseas.'[64]

Padmore's opposition to imperialism, in all of its forms, allowed him to also understand the role of the African bourgeoisie in the mainten-ance of neo-colonialism after political independence had been won. Considering this class of Africans as traitors to the African Revolution, he once wrote, 'Black capitalists are as much our enemies as white capitalists.'[65] James has argued that the independent states in Africa are led by men who are nothing more than 'functionaries' who 'sanctify the concentration of all available funds in the hands of the state, i.e., their own hands.'[66] One of the most critical opponents of the African bour-geoisie was Fanon.[67] His analysis of Pan-Africanism was permeated with an awareness of the class alliance between the African bourgeoisie and international finance capital; hence, he declared that African unity could only be achieved 'in defiance of the interests of the bourgeoisie.'[68] Touré and his party, *Parti Démocratique de Guinée*, acknowledged 'class struggle as the only dynamic and historically just step' in the struggle against imperialism.[69]

Relatedly, the Nkrumaist use of dialectical and historical materialism is another concept that can prove instructive. Although Nkrumah used, basically, the same method of analysis that others on the radical leftist use, his theoretical interpretations often deviated from some positions taken by some of the disciples of orthodox Marxism. Some of these 'deviations' revolve around issues related to racism and the national question as, for example, his rejection and revision of the Stalinist def-inition of Nationhood.[70] Even Nkrumah's insistence on an African national identity and allegiance for the African Diaspora is regarded by many Marxists as theoretical anathema.[71] Other 'deviations' are squarely in the area of philosophy as, for instance, the Nkrumaist insistence on the primary, rather than sole, existence of matter, which gives more attention to the role of ideology in transforming material conditions than does mainstream Marxism.[72]

Notwithstanding the theoretical chauvinism on the part of some Marxists, this 'deviationist' aspect of Nkrumaism shares the same sort of assimilative relationship with Pan-African thought that has been demonstrated thus far. Indeed, Dubois never swallowed Marxist theory in total, arguing that Marxism had to be 'modified so far as the Negro is concerned.'[73] James had always struggled not to let his Marxist orien-tation distort his understanding of the relationship between racism and the class struggle. Hence, while acknowledging the primacy of class struggle, he refused to succumb to the pure class analysis taken by some Marxists, once arguing that 'to neglect the racial factor as merely incidental [is] an error only less grave than to make it fundamental.'[74] Padmore, after removing his Marxist 'blinders' in 1935, counselled

Africans to 'subject Marxism to our own critical examination and see what there is in it which can be usefully applied to the conditions facing us.'[75] According to Fanon, in the context of colonialism, class exploitation and national oppression are so intertwined that 'Marxist analysis should always be slightly stretched every time we have to do with the colonial problem.'[76] Consequently, the Nkrumaist 'deviation' from doctrinaire Marxism, along the same lines carried out, and counselled, by both the predecessors and contemporaries of Nkrumah, is consistent with the type of relationship that has been demonstrated that links Nkrumaism with Pan-African thought.

Finally, Pan-Africanists have often been laudatory of the outstanding contributions African women have made to the Pan-African movement, in particular, and to the liberation struggles of African people in general. Despite occasional lapses, the ten Pan-Africanist thinkers included in this sample have certainly done so in both theory and practice, none more vigorously than Amy Jacques Garvey. As an evolving nationalist, feminist, and organizer, Amy Jacques used her journalistic prowess to rally the global community of African women to the Pan-Africanist cause: 'The doll-baby type of woman is a thing of the past, and the wide-awake woman is forging ahead prepared for all emergencies, and ready to answer any call, even if it be to face the cannons on the battlefield.'[77] Having met Nkrumah in Manchester at the Fifth Pan-Africanist Congress, and later in independent Ghana, one can only imagine the impact such a powerful woman would have on the ever evolving Ghanaian Pan-Africanist. Indeed, on the question of the role of African women in the liberation struggle, there were few women in the Pan-African movement whose words, in written and verbal form, carried as much weight as Amy Jacques' own:

> who is more deserving of admiration than the black woman, she who has borne the rigors of slavery, the deprivations consequent on a pauperized race, and the indignities heaped upon a weak and defenseless people? Yet she has suffered all with fortitude, and stands ever ready to help in the onward march to freedom and power.[78]

This experience, along with Nkrumah's observations of the immense contributions African women made to revolutionary struggle during his formative years abroad, and during the anti-colonial struggle in Ghana, may help to explain why he worked so hard to enhance the empowerment of women during his tenure in office.[79] It may also explain why this Nkrumaist statement on the role of women in the revolutionary struggle remains as inclusive, representative, and perdurable as ever: 'The degree of a country's revolutionary awareness may be measured by the political maturity of its women.'[80]

Conclusion

In his writings and speeches, drawn from the concrete conditions facing Global Africa, Nkrumah felt compelled to fill the intellectual void that had characterized revolutionary Pan-Africanism during the second half of the twentieth century:

> Social revolution must therefore have, standing firmly behind it, an intellectual revolution, a revolution in which our thinking and our philosophy are directed towards the redemption of our society. Our philosophy must find its weapons in the environment and living conditions of the African people. It is from those conditions that the intellectual content of our philosophy must be created.[81]

In this ideational investigation into the ideological antecedents, refinements, and advancements of Pan-African thought, it has been made evident that Nkrumaism lends itself, effectively, to addressing the crisis of ideological disunity within Global Africa. With an appreciation of this accomplishment, the monumental task of organizing an unorganized people—which is the only way an ideology can become a *material force*—can, along the lines advocated by Dubois, become a reality: 'When once the blacks of the United States, the West Indies, and Africa work and think together, the future of the black man in the modern world is safe.'[82] With such Pan-African cooperation, facilitated by a Pan-African ideology, the goals and objectives of the Pan-African movement can be fully realized.

Notes

1 George Padmore, *The Life of Negro Toilers*, London: Red International of Labor Unions, 1931; C.L.R. James, *History of Pan-African Revolt*, Washington, DC: Drum and Spear, 1969; W.E.B. Du Bois, *The Negro*, London: Oxford University, 1970.
2 C.L.R. James, *Nkrumah and the Ghana Revolution*, West Port, CT: Lawrence Hill, 1977, pgs. 77–78.
3 Eric Allen Engle, 'Karl Marx's Intellectual Roots in John Locke, *Postmodern Openings*, Vol. 7, September 2011, pgs. 29–37; Crystal Bartolovich, ed., *Marxism, Modernity, and the Post-Colonial Studies*, Cambridge: Cambridge

University Press, 2002; Michael Williams, 'Nkrumahism as an Ideological Embodiment of Leftist Thought Within the African World.' *Journal of Black Studies*, Vol. 15, September, pgs. 117–134.

4 Kwame Ture became one of the most ardent and influential Nkrumaists of the twentieth century as evidenced in his ideological evolution from the late 1960s to early 1970s. See Stokely Carmichael: 'Pan-Africanism—Land and Power,' *The Black Scholar*, Vol. 1, No. 1, November, 1969, pgs. 36–43; *Stokely Speaks: Black Power Back to Pan-Africanism*, New York: Random; 'Marxism-Leninism and Nkrumahism,' *The Black Scholar*, Vol. 4, No. 5, February 1973, pgs. 41–43.

5 W.E.B. DuBois, *History of Pan-African Revolt*, ibid., pgs. 5–10.

6 Marcus Garvey, *The Philosophy and Opinions of Marcus Garvey or Africa for the Africans*, London: Frank Cass, 1967, pg. 52.

7 Ibid., pg. 55.

8 Malcolm X, *The Speeches of Malcom X at Harvard*, New York: Morrow, 1968, pg. 182.

9 Stokely Carmichael, *Stokely Speaks: Black Power back to Pan-Africanism*, 1971, pgs. 111–130.

10 Kwame Nkrumah, *Class Struggle in Africa*, New York: International, 1970, pg. 87.

11 Quoted in H. Fuller, *Journey to Africa*, Chicago: Third World, 1946, pg. 70.

12 W.E.B. Du Bois, 'Africa and Africans,' *Crisis Magazine*, February 1919, Reprinted in T. Vincent, ed., *Voices of a Black Nation: Political Journalism in the Harlem Renaissance*, San Francisco: Ramparts, 1973, pg. 270.

13 Marcus Garvey, 'The African Republic and White Politics,' *The Negro World*, February 12, 1921, Reprinted in T. Vincent, ed., *Voices of a Black Nation: Political Journalism in the Harlem Renaissance*, ibid., pg. 272.

14 Marcus Garvey, 'Sacrifices for Africa,' *The Negro World*, September 24, 1926, Reprinted in T. Vincent, ed., *Voices of a Black Nation: Political Journalism in the Harlem Renaissance*, ibid., pg. 161; Marcus Garvey, *Philosophy and Opinions*, op cit., pg. 161.

15 Amy Jacques Garvey, 'The Value of Propaganda,' *The Negro World*, March 6, 1927, Reprinted in T. Vincent, ed., *Voices of a Black Nation: Political Journalism in the Harlem Renaissance*, San Francisco: Ramparts, 1973, pg. 74.

16 Malcolm X, *By Any Means Necessary*, New York: Pathfinder, pg. 136.

17 Malcolm X, *Malcolm X Speaks*, New York: Grove, 1965, pg. 57.

18 Malcolm X, *Malcolm X: Struggle for Freedom* (A filmed interview of Malcolm X in Paris), 1965, retrieved from: www.youtube.com/watch?v=_wNHjCqShs0.

19 Malcolm X, *Malcolm X Speaks*, op cit., pgs. 129–130.

20 Kwame Nkrumah, *Class Struggle in Africa*, op cit., pg. 88.

21 W.E.B. Du Bois, *The World and Africa: An Inquiry into the Part Which Africa Has Played in World History*, New York: International, 1965, pgs. 296–297.

22 Marcus Garvey, 'Prediction for Africa,' in A.J. Garvey, ed., *Garvey and Garveyism*, New York: Collier-Macmillan, 1970, pg. 169; *The Philosophy and Opinions* ..., op cit., pgs. 50, 58.

23 Sékou Touré, *The International Policy and Diplomatic Action of the Democratic Party of Guinea*, Cairo: S.O.P, 1962, pgs.154, 184.

24 Frantz Fanon, *Toward the African Revolution*, New York: Grove, 1967, pg. 187.

25 George Padmore, 1959, 'A Guide to Pan-African Socialism,' in W.H. Friedland and C.G. Roseberge, eds., *African Socialism*, Stanford, CA: Stanford University, 1964, pgs. 228–229; *Pan-Africanism or Communism*, Garden City, NY: Doubleday, 1972, pgs. xix, 356.

26 Kwame Nkrumah, *Africa Must Unite*, New York: International, 1963, pgs. 214–215; *Revolutionary Path*, New York: International, 1973, pg. 307.

27 W.E.B. Du Bois, *The World and Africa*, op cit., pg. 296.

28 Kwame Nkrumah, *Africa Must Unite*, op cit.; *Handbook of Revolutionary Warfare: A Guide to the Armed Phase of the African Revolution*, New York: International, 1968; *Class Struggle in Africa*, op cit., pgs. 87–88.

29 Kwame Nkrumah, *Consciencism*, op cit., pgs. 70, 78–79.

30 Marcus Garvey, *Philosophy and Opinions* ..., op cit., pgs. 71, 84–88; Sékou Touré, 'A Dialectical Approach to Culture,' in R. Chrisman and N. Hare, eds., *Black Thought: The Best from the Black Scholar*, Indianapolis, IN: Bobbs-Merrill, pgs. 3–11; Frantz Fanon, *Towards the African Revolution*, op cit., pg. 38; Frantz Fanon, *Black Skin, White Masks*, New York: Grove, 1967.

31 Marcus Garvey, *Philosophy and Opinions*, ibid., pg. 27.

32 Julius Nyerere, *Ujamaa: Essays in Socialism*, New York: Oxford, 1962, pgs. 1–12.

33 Kwame Nkrumah, *Consciencism*, op cit., pg. 79; see also pgs. 68, 70, 78–79.

34 C.L.R. James, *Nkrumah and the Ghana Revolution*, op. cit., pg. 62.

35 Marcus Garvey, *Philosophy and Opinions*, op cit., pg. 111.

36 A.J. Garvey, *Garvey and Garveyism*, op cit., pgs. 145–147.

37 Marcus Garvey, *Philosophy and Opinions* ..., op cit., pg. 69.

38 Ibid.

39 Ibid., pg. 53.

40 Ibid., pg. 52.

41 Malcolm X, *Malcolm X: Struggle for Freedom*, op cit.; *Malcolm X Speaks*, op cit., pgs. 65, 68–69, 121, 149.

42 Malcolm X, *By Any Means Necessary*, op cit., pg. 181.

43 Kwame Nkrumah, 'African Socialism Revisited,' in *Revolutionary Path*, op cit., 1970, pgs. 438–445.

44 Julius Nyerere, *Ujamaa*, op cit., pgs. 6–8.

45 Walter Rodney, *How Europe Underdeveloped Africa*, Washington, DC: Howard University, 1974, pgs. 40–83.

46 Leo Zeilig, ed., *Class Struggle and Resistance in Africa*, Chicago: Haymarket Books, 2008; Dieter Neubert, *Inequality, Socio-Cultural Differentiation, and Social Structures in Africa: Beyond Class*, Springer Link, 2019, Immanuel

Wallerstein, 'Class and Class Conflict in Contemporary Africa,' *Canadian Journal of African Studies*, Vol. 7, No. 3, Special Issue: Social Stratification in Africa, 1973, pgs. 375–380.

47 Kwame Nkrumah, *Revolutionary Path*, op cit., pg. 441.

48 Ibid., pgs. 440–441.

49 Kwame Nkrumah, *Class Struggle in Africa*, op cit., pg. 10.

50 Ibid.

51 Ibid., pgs. 10, 12.

52 Ibid., pg. 65.

53 See Panaf, *Kwame Nkrumah*, Panaf: London, pgs. 234–237.

54 Kwame Nkrumah, *Revolutionary Path*, op cit., pgs. 421–428.

55 Kwame Nkrumah, *Class Struggle in Africa*, op cit.

56 Kwame Nkrumah, *Revolutionary Path*, op cit., pgs. 428.

57 Stokely Carmichael, *Stokely Speaks*, op cit., pg. 179.

58 Ibid., pg. 121.

59 Kwame Nkrumah, *Class Struggle in Africa*, op cit., pg. 29.

60 Kwame Nkrumah, *Revolutionary Path*, op cit., pg. 423.

61 *World and Africa*, op cit., pg. 309; George Padmore, 'A Guide to Pan-African Socialism,' in W.H. Friedland and C.G. Roseberge, eds., *African Socialism*, op cit., pg. 237; C.L.R. James, *Nkrumah and the Ghana Revolution*, op cit., pgs. 14–15; Stokely Carmichael, *Stokely Speaks*, op cit., pg. 115.

62 Ibid., pgs. 205, 210–212.

63 Kwame Nkrumah, *Class Struggle*, op cit., pg. 63.

64 W.E.B. Du Bois, *The World and Africa*, op cit., pg. 309.

65 George Padmore, 'A Guide to Pan-African Socialism,' in W.H. Friedland and C.G. Roseberge, eds., *African Socialism*, op cit., pg. 237.

66 C.L.R. James, *Nkrumah and the Ghana Revolution*, op cit., pgs. 14–15.

67 Frantz Fanon, *The Wretched of the Earth*, New York: Grove, 1963, pgs. 148–205.

68 Ibid., pg. 164.

69 Sékou Touré, *Strategy and Tactics of the Revolution*, Conakry: Press Office, 1977, pg. 277.

70 Kwame Nkrumah, *Class Struggle*, op cit., pg. 88.

71 B. Amponsem, 'Pan-Africanism Makes Transition,' *The Guardian: The Independent Radical Newspaper*, July 25, 1979, pg. 17. See also Parts II and III of this same article in the *Guardian*, August 15, 1979, pg. 17, and August 22, 1979, pg. 17.

72 Kwame Nkrumah, *Consciencism*, op cit., pgs. 34, 84; Progress, *The Fundamentals of Marxist-Leninist Philosophy*, Moscow: Progress, 1974, pg. 72.

73 W.E.B. Du Bois, 'Marxism and the Negro Question,' *The Crisis Magazine, May 1933*, Reprinted in T. Vincent, ed., *Voices of a Black Nation: Political Journalism in the Harlem Renaissance*, op cit., pg. 215.

74 C.L.R. James, *The Black Jacobins: Tourssaint L'Ouverture and the San Domingo Revolution*, New York: Vintage, Second Edition, Revised, 1963, pg.

283; see Tony Martin, 'C.L.R. James and the Race/Class Question,' *Race*, Vol. XIV, No. 2, pgs. 183–193 for an informative discussion on this issue.

75 George Padmore, 'A Guide to Pan-African Socialism,' op cit., pg. 227.

76 Frantz Fanon, *The Wretched of the Earth*, op cit., pg. 40.

77 Amy Jacques Euphemia Garvey, 'Women as Leaders,' *The Negro World*, October 25, 1925.

78 Ibid.

79 Abayomi Azikiwe, 'Revising the Role of Women in Kwame Nkrumah's Ghana: Pan-Africanism, Gender, Emancipation, and the Meaning of Socialist Development,' Pan-African News Wire, August 28, 2016, retrieved from: https://newsghana.com.gh/viewpoint-revisiting-the-role-of-women-in-kwame-nkrumahs-ghana/.

80 Kwame Nkrumah, *Handbook*, op cit., pg. 91.

81 Kwame Nkrumah, *Consciencism: Philosophy and Ideology of Decolonization*, New York: Monthly Review, 1964, pg. 78.

82 W.E.B. Du Bois, *The World and Africa*, op cit., pg. 374.

3 Continental unification as a prerequisite to African development

The potential benefits of Africa's land, labour, and mineral resources, all of which exist in abundance, can only be fully realized when Africa unites and the fruits of its humongous resources, both human and physical, are shared equitably among the masses of its people. In short, the African people, at home and abroad, can only develop to their fullest potential, and reap the material and immaterial benefits of their inheritance, when the continent becomes one united socialist nation. Nkrumah said it best:

> The optimum zone of development for the African people is the entire continent of Africa. Until there is an All-African Union Government pursuing socialist policies, and planning the economic development of Africa as a whole, the standard of living of the African masses will remain low, and they will continue to suffer from neocolonialist exploitation and the oppression of the indigenous bourgeois.[1]

Below is a detailed summary of exactly how the Nkrumaist call for African unification will benefit the continent and its people.

African resources

The incredible amount of Africa's rich, variegated wealth has been well documented and remains an indubitable fact.[2] As the second largest continent in the world, its 30 million square kilometres of land surface holds enough mineral wealth, agricultural potential, and (fresh) water reserves to meet the material needs of the vast and growing population of Africans many times over. However, these resources do not exist, equally, among Africa's 55 balkanized sates. In other words, the main features of Africa's topography, geography, and demography show no relationship

DOI: 10.4324/9781003224990-4

to the manner in which Africa has been carved up by its colonial masters. Thus, while some countries, like the Democratic Republic of the Congo (DRC), are huge and endowed with an abundance of various natural resources, others, like the Gambia, are tiny and seriously bereft.

But why should this be so? The majority of people who inhabit the Gambia today—along with those currently living in Senegal, Mauritania, Guinea, Burkina Faso, Niger, La Cote d'Ivoire, and Mali—are direct descendants of those same people who were an integral part of the ancient Mali Empire between the thirteenth and fifteenth centuries.[3] Led by such prominent leaders as Sundiata Keita and the famous Mansa Musa, the Mali Empire, at its peak, stretched across 1.2 million square kilometres of West Africa's finest water bodies, rainforests, tropical grasslands, and mountain plateaus. Known famously for its immense deposits and mining of gold, Mali prospered largely because of extensive trade within and outside its borders.[4] Why, then, should the people living in the Gambia today be denied the inheritance of their ancestry simply because they find themselves locked in a tiny artificially created state, barely 48 kilometres wide, with hardly any natural resources? And much the same can be said of many other states on the continent. The minuscule, resource-poor state of Burundi, located in Africa's Great Lakes Region, is another example: its people are direct descendants of an erstwhile kingdom several times larger than the current borders of Burundi.[5] Indeed, this external disruption of the state formation process in Africa is representative of the tragic history of Africa's colonial past.

Yet Africa's abundance *has* to benefit Africans as a whole, continentally and globally, and not those who, from abroad, continue to divide and plunder it in the interests of imperialism or those, among the indigenous bourgeoisie, who are amassing an astonishing amount of personal wealth (in both the private and public sectors).[6] However, this can only be done when these resources are managed and shared, continentally, within the context of one African socialist nation. But first we should have some idea of the exact extent of this abundance as it is scattered, unevenly, across the continent. Below is a summary of the major resources of Africa, centred around five main related areas: mineral wealth, agriculture potential, freshwater availability, renewable energy, and human resources.

Mineral wealth

The mineral wealth of Africa, much of which is still undiscovered and unharnessed, is prodigious in both its depth and diversity. Just one country, alone, the DRC, has an estimated $24 trillion in mineral reserves, including gold, diamonds, copper, cobalt, tin, tungsten, zinc, manganese, magnesium, uranium, niobium, and silver.[7] Moreover, most of Africa's mineral resources fall within the category of strategic importance as defined by the United States and other nations of the Industrial North. This is because of (1) the critical role these resources play in the industrial and military development of these nations, and (2) the fact that these resources are either not found or produced in these countries or, if they are, the amount available or produced pales in comparison to the amount found and produced in Africa.

More than 50 percent of the world's *diamonds*, for example, come from just five countries in Africa: Botswana, Angola, South Africa, Namibia, and the DRC. The continent's *oil* output is equivalent to that of Saudi Arabia, the largest oil producer in the world; its *gas* output is twice that of Qatar's own. Sixty per cent of the world's *cobalt*, an element indispensable in the manufacturing of smart phones, laptops, tablets, electric cars, gas turbines, and jet engines, originates in the DRC; huge deposits can also be found in Zambia, Morocco, and Botswana. Nearly 80 percent of one of the rarest metals in the world, *platinum*, the corrosion resister, is produced in South Africa and Zimbabwe. *Coal*, which heats homes and produces electricity around the world, is found in large deposits in South Africa, Egypt, Mozambique, Botswana, Malawi, Niger, Swaziland, Zimbabwe, Zambia, and Tanzania. A whopping 98 percent of the known reserves of *chromium*, a metal of critical use in high temperature applications, including the manufacturing of stainless steel, is located in South Africa and Zimbabwe; no aerospace or defence industry can survive without it either. Only *uranium* can enrich the fuel used in nuclear power plants, 1.2 million metric tons of which exists in Africa, viz., Namibia, Niger, Botswana, Tanzania, and South Africa; no other continent, save for Australia, comes close to having that amount of reserves. South Africa, alone, produces more *manganese* than any continent, let alone country, standing as the world leader with 6.2 million metric tons; combined with Gabon and Ghana, these three manganese giants produce more than 8.3 million metric tons of this invaluable metal used in the production of iron and steel. The soaring global demand for laptops, cell phones, and a variety of other electronic devises would not be met were it not for the existence of columbite–tantalite, *coltan* for short, of which nearly 70 percent of the world's known reserves can be found in the DRC. And finally there is *gold*, always ranked as one of the most valuable mineral resources in the world, a precious metal being produced, in abundance, in South Africa, Ghana, Burkina Faso, Mali, Guinea and more than 20 other balkanized states in Africa.

Incredibly, the above inventory is only a partial listing. There are also vast untapped reserves of radium, iron ores, copper, lead, zinc, tin, titanium, antimony, tantalum, germanium, lithium, phosphates, and bauxite, among others, located underneath the African terrain. With proper management and continental planning, there is no reason why the ordinary citizens of Africa cannot benefit, entirely, from the mineral resources of their continent, especially when these benefits are shared, equitably, along socialist lines. These resources, existing randomly across Africa's balkanized borders, many of which are controlled by foreign nationals, have often been the source of conflicts throughout the post-colonial period. Sadly, this has been the case on both interstate and intrastate levels, especially in cases involving oil and gas rights.[8] This, in fact, is what resource-poor countries around the world have been doing from times immemorial: going to war to acquire and/or protect valuable scarce resources. But instead of fighting over them, and letting the corporate magnates of the Industrial North (and their domestic counterparts) continue siphoning them for their own private pecuniary gains, plans should be well underway to meet the Pan-African imperative: to incorporate the exploitation of these mineral resources into an integrative, continent-wide strategic plan for the full-scale industrialization of Africa for the benefit of Africans. Indeed, until Africans start polishing their own diamonds, refining their own gold, and producing, with the use of their own cobalt and coltan, cell phones and lap top computers, *in Africa*, in their own factories and plants, it would be far better to simply leave these metals in the ground. After all, maintaining the status quo will simply mean continuing to lose, annually, the estimated $50 billion of illicit finance flows and unpaid taxes to the Global North, much of which comes from Africa's natural resources.[9]

Agriculture potential

Although Africa is largely arid and semi-arid, with the Sahara Desert, alone, larger than the continental United States, its agricultural potential is one of the greatest, if not *the* greatest, in the world. According to the Food and Agricultural Organization (FAO) of the UN, the cultivable land of Africa, excluding its forests, is more than three times greater than the land currently being cultivated.[10] In numerical terms, the ratio is staggering: only approximately 179 out of 632 million hectares of Africa's cultivable land is being cultivated! In fact, Africa has nearly 70 percent of the remaining arable land in the entire world which, when properly utilized and developed, will not only feed Africa's growing population, but much of the world as well.

Yet, incredibly, Africa's annual bill for food imports, excluding fish, is a whopping $35 billion![11] And this is not because there are too few farmers in Africa farming on the one-third of Africa's cultivable land. After all, more than 70 percent of mainland Africans are engaged in farming, compared to less than 5 percent of their counterparts in the Global North; however, in the case of the former, their farms produce barely 40 percent of their potential.[12] All of this, of course, accounts for the millions of malnourished women, men, and children that populate much of Africa. Fortunately, this agricultural crisis—of food scarcity amid an abundance of potential—is solvable. And while the solutions to solving this crisis are all centred on the Pan-African imperative, let it suffice, for now, to draw the following conclusion: Endowed with a wide diversity of agro-ecological zones, Africa has a huge tropical farming belt—found mostly in its western, eastern, and central regions—that has the biophysical capacity to feed all of Africa, including those areas where the soil is either unsuitable or too fragile to grow food. With proper continental planning, as discussed below, hunger will no longer exist in Africa, that is, as long as this potential is realized along socialist lines.

Freshwater availability

While more than 300 million people in Africa live in a relatively water-scarce environment, Africa, as whole, is not a water scare continent. On the contrary, scattered throughout much of Africa is 63 river basins, many of which share boundaries with several nation-states; there are also several nation-states that have multiple river basins within their borders. And despite the very real threat to these water bodies from global warming and nefarious mining activities, Africa is not bereft of fresh water. In fact, in addition to the huge reservoir of surface water, Africa's *underground* water reserves are more than 100 times greater than its renewal freshwater resources; and while all of this water is not easily accessible, much of it is, as Muammar Qadhafi so bravely demonstrated with his 'Great Man-Made River Project' built right in the heart of the Sahara Desert. In fact, studies show that much of Africa's groundwater can be made available all year-round, making it possible to farm even during the dry season.[13]

Instead, Africa's water crisis revolves around the very low level of water resource utilization in which water is accessed and distributed throughout the continent. Astonishingly, only 5 percent of Africa's renewable water resources are currently being utilized.[14] However, with a Union Government of Africa committed to continental integrative management, there is no reason why Africa's water resources cannot be used to meet the agricultural, health, and industrial needs of the continent as a whole.[15] Indeed, when droughts hit (accompanied by desertification), it is rarely the single balkanized states that are struck; instead, it is the continent, or large swaths of the continent, which are affected. Such conditions necessitate the need for a Pan-African recovery strategy. Conversely, with the implementation of proper Pan-African policies, there is no reason why the enormous agricultural potential available in Africa's flood plains—adjacent to the Nile, Zambezi, Niger, Senegal, and Congo rivers, and many other smaller ones—cannot be realized. A flood-based system of farming—entailing flood control, water retention, and drainage management—would result in these 300 million hectares of (largely neglected) sub-Saharan land becoming a continental breadbasket for the teeming millions of African children who go hungry every year.

Renewable energy

The shortage of power access and the poor quality of power supply throughout the continent undermines and inhibits industrial development in Africa. Despite the rapidly growing demands for reliable energy, we have severe problems in both generating and transmitting it throughout the continent (where nearly 70 percent of the population is without reliable power supply).[16] This is especially true in areas outside of major cities where the vast majority of people still live. Sadly, still, the overwhelming majority of power supply in Africa is sourced through environmentally damaging, non-renewable fossil fuels, viz., coal, oil, and natural gas. Ironically, the primary effect of these fuels on the planet, global warming, is having a devastating impact on Africa, not least of which include, minimally, an increase in floods and droughts, decrease in water supply, reduction in crop yields, destruction of ecosystems, lowering the quality of life, and exacerbating problems of national security.[17]

Fortunately, Africa's renewable energy resources are immense. However, they can only be properly developed with continent-wide integrative planning and the abundance of investment funding that only a Union Government of Africa can provide. Solar energy, wind power, hydropower, geothermal energy, biomass, and biofuel—the six leading sources of green energy in Africa—can only be effectively and efficiently harnessed within the context of their topographical location in Africa. The imperialist-imposed, artificial division of Africa should not, as it has been since its inception, distort our vision on this issue! In short, when we think and plan continentally, the green energy revolution, which has already begun in Africa, becomes significantly more affordable and manageable. With a continental energy master plan, not only will regional grid integration become possible, but also the benefits of economy of scale will result in a significant decrease in the costs of producing renewable energy.[18]

There are a number of projects that have taken off and been in place for years now, including the West African Power Pool, the Grand Inga Hydroelectric project in the Congo Basin, Africa Clean Energy Corridor, and many others. However, most of these projects rely heavily, if not exclusively, on the donor institutions and neo-colonizing nations of the Global North, including the European Union (EU), the UN, the United States, World Bank (WB), and others, whose pecuniary interests often prevent these projects from benefiting the people whose renewable resources are being exploited.[19] Only a Union Government of Africa—considering the near ineptness of the African Union (AU) in addressing any of these challenges—can repair this anomaly while assuring that these projects, which are usually regional in scope, can encompass the entire continent and its people.

Human resources

The most important resource of any nation is its people. An Nkrumaist adage, here, is apropos: 'There is no force, however formidable, that a united people cannot overcome.'[20] This truth, however, is best realized when people are properly trained, educated, and organized. Certainly, Africa's physical resources, as abundant as they are, would have little or no meaning if it were not for the physical strength and intellectual ingenuity of its people who are capable of uncovering, extracting, transforming, and harnessing these resources for human use and consumption. In this regard, the demographic situation in Africa today, where some of the highest birth rates in the world are recorded, gives reason to pause. With a population of over 1.3 billion people, Africa is faced with either an enormous opportunity for development, especially considering its potential market size, or a very dangerous precipice for untold human suffering.

It all depends on how it is managed.[21] Indeed, the concept of over-population, of which Africa is so frequently accused, is entirely relative. The number of people in Africa, per square kilometre, is actually very low compared to much of the Global North.[22] Had Africa's rural areas not been so grossly exploited *and* neglected under colonial and post-colonial periods of underdevelopment, Africa's overpopulated urban centres today would not be so overwhelmed in their inability to meet the social consumption needs of energy, sanitation, housing, education, transport, healthcare, and food of its citizenry. Still, Africa's rapid urban migration, which exacerbates Africa's so-called population crisis, should not be a problem at all. On the contrary, the teeming millions of people who are pouring into Africa's small towns and growing cities could easily contribute to Africa's sustainable development. The market demand they create, alone, is enough to drive the industrial development of the entire continent. However, if the wealth from Africa's raw materials, mineral resources, and exploited labour continues to flow outside, instead of inside, there will be no resources available to invest in the production of the services and goods required to meet this gigantic and growing demand. In essence, with an end to imperialist plundering and the implementation of careful continental planning, African population pressures will, in time, serve to enhance the realization of Pan-African goals and objectives.

Another critical, and very exciting, component of this demographic is what some have called Africa's 'Secret Weapon,' the African Diaspora, whose current population is over 200 million.[23] As indicated in Chapter 1, this community has always impacted, or been impacted by, developments that have taken place on the African mainland. Indeed, neither community can be properly understood without understanding the common history and aspirations of them both. This is the case today as much as it was centuries ago when peoples of African descent began leaving the continent, either by force or volition, including: (1) those who migrated before the Arab and European slave trades; (2) those who were forced out and enslaved because of those 'trades'; and (3) those second, third, and multiple generation descendants of Africans who left in search of *greener pastures* during and after the colonial period. With this latter group of Diasporans, what better way to arrest the enormous brain drain that has been crippling Africa for generations than by creating industrial-size opportunities for Africa's youth to expend its creativity, ingenuity, and inventiveness, *in Africa*, in solving African problems? In this way, men and women like Dr. Ashitey Trebi-Ollennu, the brilliant Ghanaian engineer who served as the lead engineer in designing the Mars Rover Robot for NASA, can stay home, anywhere in Africa, and fulfil his highest aspirations.[24] So, too, will the thousands of doctors, nurses, and lab technician, and a wide variety of other professionals be inclined to stay home and serve Africa's health care (and various other) needs. In short, the African population of those at home and abroad make up a formidable (1.5 billion) force, capable of solving *any* of the multifaceted and multilayered problems facing the African continent.

Another decisive part of the Diaspora dynamic is the issue of remittances. Billions of dollars and euros are remitted to Africa, annually, willy-nilly, by a significant segment of the African Diaspora. These funds, for years, have been making a huge contribution to the economies of many states in Africa, in some cases amounting to over 10 percent of their GDPs.[25] However, imagine the greater impact these enormous funds, most of which end up in the hands of private individuals and families, would have if at least a portion of it would be issued as Diasporic Bonds by, say, the 'Great Bank of Africa?' These are bonds that would be officially earmarked to policies and measures enacted by a Union Government of Africa whose main focus would be on the integrative development of the entire continent.[26] What conscious person within the African Diaspora, who can afford to, would not contribute funds to Africa's development once Africa is led by responsible women and men, with vision, whose sole aim is the development of the continent? Moreover, these bonds, while earning income for those who purchase them, would have terms for Africa vastly superior to the financially draining conditions tied to Euro Bonds.[27] They would be purchased by Africans in the Diaspora whose primary aim is simple: providing support for causes in health, education, agriculture, science and technology, and the general welfare of the continent. If managed properly, the opportunities for economic growth and development would be incalculable.

Africans in the Diaspora of various historical backgrounds have made, and will continue to make, various other contributions. This is why, at the dawn of independence, Nkrumah was so insistent on attracting that community to Ghana.[28] As an efflorescing Pan-Africanist, this is why he also wrote, years later, that, 'All peoples of African descent, whether they live in North or South America, the Caribbean, or in any other part of the world are African and belong to the African nation.'[29] Orchestrating the synergy of African peoples at home and abroad into one powerful force, as Marcus Garvey and countless others lived and died for, remains an integral part of the Pan-African imperative.

Investment capital

What nation has ever developed by begging other nations and international donor agencies for loans and investment capital, especially if these loans and investments are acquired on terms that so disproportionately favour the donor nations and capital investors? The answer is simple: none! However, as long as Africa remains in its balkanized state, what choice does it have but to continue meeting with donor nations and institutions, state by state, hat in hand, accepting agreements that are so egregiously lopsided and unfair? This degrading condition Africa finds itself engulfed in is understandable: billions of dollars are looted from Africa, legally and illegally, by wealthy individuals and multinational corporations (MNCs) every year.[30] In fact, in the last 50 years, experts in the field of international trade and finance have shown that—primarily through trade misinvoicing—Africa has lost over $1 trillion dollars from unpaid taxes on the underreporting of profits earned.[31] Furthermore, through tax havens and tax concessions, often facilitated, willingly and unwillingly, by Africa's indigenous political elite, billions more have flowed, and continue to flow, out of Africa every year.[32] And not to be outdone by these (mostly) legal measures, illegal logging, fishing, poaching, and mining account for billions more![33]

Yet, Africa needs vast amounts of money, multiple billions of dollars, annually, to maintain and build new roads and bridges; to produce medicines and provide health care; to train teachers and educate children; to provide clean water, remove waste, and protect its environment; and to eradicate hunger and eliminate poverty. However, this problem, a structural manifestation of a late, moribund, globalized capitalism, cannot be solved by just one country. Africa must achieve genuine political unity to not only put an end to this plundering, but also to collect this vast amount of wealth to finance large-scale (agricultural and industrial) projects that require it. Even today, excluding the billions in tax revenue not being paid to African governments across the continent, Africa generates $540 billion in tax revenue per year. And this amount, alone, is large enough to solve Africa's energy crisis which, according to experts, requires approximately $90–120 billion, annually, to solve.[34] In other words, less than 20 percent of the taxes we *are* able to wrestle from individual and corporate taxpayers in Africa would be enough to light up and power all of Africa (if only we pool this continent-wide tax revenue). Imagine the impact this would have on Africa's economic growth rate. As in the case with China, it would remain in double digits.[35] Much the same could be said with the total amount of foreign reserves held, collectively, in African federal banks across the continent—well over half a trillion dollars.[36] This amount is relatively small, in global terms, representing less than 5 percent of the world's foreign reserves. However, in terms of what it could do for Africa, if pooled and earmarked for planned, continental development, is inestimable. This is the type of money required for the large-scale production of heavy, sophisticated equipment designed to produce cars, trucks, tractors, roads, bridges, trains, ships, aircraft, and other basic items required for sustainable development in the twenty-first century.

Optimal market size

The purchasing power of the African continent is immense. With a total population of more than 1.3 billion people, characterized by swelling numbers of middle income earners ready to purchase a nearly unlimited spectrum of goods and services, Africa is recognized as one of the fastest growing consumer markets in the world.[37] Consumer expenditures reached $1.4 trillion in 2015 and are expected to reach $2.1 trillion by 2025. Incredibly, if Africa's current population trends continue, by 2050 its total population will be greater than the populations of China and India combined! Imagine, then, what its total consumer expenditures would be in less than 30 years! However, as it stands now, the 55 balkanized states of Africa turn this remarkable purchasing power over, free of charge, to the heavily industrialized countries of the developed world. Africa simply does not trade with itself anymore, denying itself huge employment opportunities and gigantic economies of scale—in short, the opportunity to create large-scale factories and plants capable of producing the goods and services needed to meet the consumer demands of its people.

In Ghana, for example, one can easily purchase Heineken Beer (brewed in the Netherlands), Becks Beer (brewed in Germany), and Miller Beer (brewed in the United States). However, try to find Flag Beer, from its neighbour, Togo, and you will never find it; nor will the Togolese find *in Togo*, Club Beer, Star Beer, or Gulder Beer, all brewed in Ghana! Unlike Cuba, which has suffered for the past 60 years from an *externally* imposed trade embargo, Africa, during this same time span, has, with *help*, imposed one on itself. A similar absurdity can be illustrated in the amount of money used in the purchase of imported rice in Ghana, currently over $500,000,000 per annum.[38] How can one country with the climatic conditions and soil quality to produce enough rice to meet the demands of the entire West African sub-region (of over 360 million people) be reduced to wasting valuable foreign reserves on purchasing rice from the United States and Asia? And you have to taste just how delicious Ghanaian rice is, especially its brown rice variety, to really appreciate this tragedy. These examples in Ghana, unfortunately, are only the tip of the iceberg. Other examples abound throughout the continent.[39]

And while there is reason for (slight) optimism in the recently signed agreement establishing the African Continental Free Trade Area (AfCFTA),[40] there is also reason for (grave) concern. With less than 40 countries having 'Deposited their Instruments of Ratification' with the AU, how long will it take to implement this Agreement, an Agreement that will be implemented in phases, some phases of which are still subject to negotiation? There are also articles in this Agreement that allow for member states to (1) avoid, or waive, being required to abide by the obligations of this Agreement and (2) protect their infant industries if it is in the interest of a particular nation-state to do so.[41] Indeed, the soft and indecisive language used throughout this Agreement—for example, 'consider, promote, collaborate, recommend, cooperate and propose,'—is reminiscent of the liberal wording used in the Charter of the Organization of African Unity,[42] an organization whose liberal approach to African liberation and unity served to inhibit it from making as significant a contribution as it could have.[43] However, the more concerning problem facing AfCFTA is the same problem that lies at the very root of Africa's gigantic malaise—the absence of a Union Government of Africa, guided by socialist principles, whose primary purpose is to reclaim ownership of Africa's mineral wealth from foreign looters, while marshalling the political and economic unity and liberation of its people.[44]

Protectionism and state intervention

Without exception, every developed nation, that is, every nation with an advanced technological and industrial infrastructure, has relied, in one form or another, on state intervention and protectionism to facilitate and fuel its development. Britain, the first benefactor of the mid-eighteenth century Industrial Revolution, provides the earliest example of this recurrent lesson in economic history. Its global manufacturing dominance by the nineteenth century was squarely rooted in nearly two centuries, earlier, of mercantilist policies, most notably in its Navigation Acts.[45] Indeed, its North American colonies found it next to impossible to add value to anything they produced, or to trade with any other country besides England. The full arsenal of protectionist weapons (of tariffs, duties, subsidies, and taxes) were used against its colonial subjects to protect British manufactures.

Colonial rebellion against such exploitative policies, quite obviously, would only result, and did, culminating in the defeat and expulsion of the British and the birth of a new republic, the United States. Yet, before the ink had dried on the constitution of the new independent republic, the very *second* bill ever signed by its new president, George Washington, was titled, 'Duties on Merchandise Imported into the United States.' This bill, which was ratified by the new congress in 1789, initiated a decades-long series of protectionist and interventionist legislation that enabled the United States to become the manufacturing powerhouse that it is today, especially in the production of weapons of war.[46] Industrialized Europe and Japan followed an identical path: each of their various governments intervened during their pre-industrial stage of development to ensure the economic success of their manufacturing sectors.[47] And nothing much has changed over the past 50 years, as demonstrated in the state-driven economic policies that are responsible for the accelerated development of the so-called Asian Tigers and, most notably, the People's Republic of China.[48] Even today, the World Trade Organization (WTO), whose rules and regulations underdeveloped countries are obliged to follow, has little control over the industrialized giants of the world. These predator nations continue, with impunity, to impose quotas, provide subsidies, and raise tariff levels whenever it suits their interests.

Clearly, only a Union Government of Africa, backed by the power that comes from speaking with one voice, will have the authority to free the African economy from the shackles of the absurdities of neo-liberalism. How else will African poultry farmers compete with their EU competitors who benefit from huge subsidies in the form of chicken feed (which accounts for a significant amount of the production costs of poultry farming)?[49] How will African textile manufacturing ever survive without import restrictions placed on those cheap, second-hand clothes pouring into the continent from the United States? How will African tomato growers sell their crops before they rot on the ground—as they do, routinely—without government intervention in support of industrial manufacturing of canned tomato paste and other tomato-based by-products? Do Italian tomato paste factories, whose products fill the shelves of African supermarkets, rely on tomatoes grown in Africa? Of course not; nor should they. The list of damages resulting from an unprotected economy, deprived of state supervision and planning, left to the vagaries of unfettered market forces, is endless! Once united, no one, including the IMF, WB, WTO, or any predator nation, no matter how powerful, will be able to demand that Africa open its ports and harbours, unprotected.

Bargaining power

The balkanized states of Africa are always at a disadvantage when bargaining, separately, with the stronger industrial nations of Europe,

Asia, and North America. Yet, African Heads of States are fond of, each year, visiting China, the EU, or whichever predator nation or institution invites them, to negotiate deals that are rarely in the best (long-term) interest of their respective countries. In short, African countries enter the bargaining arena, alone, with far too few chips with which to play. They are either too small, too weak, or too indebted to refuse signing agreements that fail to provide their countries with economic advantages to assist in their development.[50] The Economic Partnership Agreements that African countries, and some of their Caribbean counterparts, have been signing are glaring examples of this.[51] By signing agreements with EU countries that give them duty-free access to African markets, African countries find it very difficult to (1) produce agricultural and non-agricultural products that can successfully compete with cheaper European products; (2) establish coterminous trade relations with non-European nations, especially in Asia and Latin America; and (3) coordinate the economic integration of the continent.[52]

The negotiations between African countries and MNCs produce results that are equally as harmful.[53] In addition to the exploitation of labour, environmental damage, and health and safety risks they often subject poor nations to, MNCs are literally getting away with murder. This can be seen by studying the fine print on some of the MOUs the two parties sign. Tax-free holidays, 90-year leases, duty-free imports, unbridled repatriation of profits, interest-free bank loans, and lopsided profit-sharing agreements are just some of the debilitating giveaways African countries have been offering, on bended knees, to woo the MNCs to invest in their separate countries.

However, the moment the Union Government of Africa sits at the negotiating table representing its 1.5 billion people, the ball game will become completely different. Size matters! So, too, do the critical mineral resources a united Africa will have at its disposal, capable of providing enough leverage to open up a treasure-trove of unimaginable advantages. Bargaining from a position of strength, Africa will be able to make demands on the EU, China, the United States, and foreign direct investors that will have to be considered, including, but not limited to, technology transfer, value-added investments, and joint partnerships that allow both sides to gain fairly.

Common currency

The realization of a common currency for Africa is not actually one of the benefits of African Unity. Instead, the establishment of a single African currency is one of the necessary preconditions for the full-scale economic integration of the continent. It will serve as a major facilitator to enhance intra-African trade and commerce, mainly through these three primary accrued opportunities: (1) the elimination of transaction costs when converting multiple currencies; (2) the removal of exchange rate volatility and fluctuations; and (3) the provision of transparency in pricing goods and services. These benefits, when achieved, will allow intra-African trade, perforce, to skyrocket, creating the conditions for economic growth and development throughout the continent. And despite the discouraging advice from a minority of naysaying pundits, several studies have substantiated the veracity of this argument.[54]

Indeed, if the benefits of a single currency, on a continental scale, were not as significant as is being suggested above, the Euro would have been jettisoned years ago by countries with economies as varied as those 27 nations belonging to the EU. To its credit, nay, for its survival, the EU has found a way for this to work. Hence, under EU control, economic giants like Germany, with a population of over 83 million people, and with a GDP of nearly four trillion dollars, has synchronized its economy with much smaller countries, like Estonia, whose population of barely 1.3 million people carry on their affairs with a GDP of less than 1 percent of the German total. And it is the Euro that is expediting this entire process of European integration, managed, more than ever before, by the centralization of banking policy of the European Central Bank.[55]

The *synchronization* of the 55 African economies, then, is the greatest challenge to achieving a single African currency under the current political division of Africa. This is because the financial benchmarks each of the countries in Africa would have to meet in order to achieve the level of synchronization required for single currency usage are not realistic targets—not for a continent that was as thoroughly divided and colonized as was Africa. How long would it take for each of the 55 countries in Africa to meet the following standard criteria for single currency usage among economically diverse countries: (1) 3 percent or less budget deficits; (2) single digit average annual inflation rates; (3) central bank financing of budgets no less than 10 percent of previous year's tax revenue; and (4) availability of not less than three months' worth of total reserves of imports. The answer is simple: too long, if not, forever (given their current neo-colonized condition). Instead of each separate country concentrating on meeting these (and other) criteria, the Union Government of Africa could be investing in large poles of economic development throughout the continent. In every region of Africa, these poles of sectoral growth would be built around key industries, such as automotive, agribusiness, electronics, steel, transportation, and so on.

This would, in turn, engender an ancillary pool of economic activity, compelling and complementing the creation of a single African currency, ensuring the smooth flow of supply chain activity across the (artificial) borders of the continent.[56] In short, Africa must unite and begin planning for opportunities of growth now, and not wait, indefinitely, for opportunities to fall into its (divided) lap.

Continental planning

Nearly all of what has been (and will be) discussed in this chapter falls within the parameters of continental planning. Without a doubt, continental planning intersects with practically every phase of development in Africa and is the cornerstone upon which all of the major challenges facing Africa can be addressed and solved. This is because there are no major problems facing Africa that do not transcend the artificial boundaries that have engulfed the continent. In short, the very survival of Africa and its people requires significant levels of continental planning in areas as vast as agriculture, industry, health, and biodiversity, to name but a few. Below is a brief summary of how these four areas can be impacted, positively, by continental planning.

Agriculture

Miraculously, less than 6 percent of African farmland is irrigated. And given the deleterious impact climate change has been having on Africa's rain-fed agricultural systems, continental planning in this area is more urgent than ever before.[57] Fortunately, as discussed above, the availability of freshwater resources in Africa is abundant. And again, this water can be made available for the millions of African farmers, best, by developing a coordinated plan of action that involves large swaths of the continent. Unfortunately, rather than planning on a continental basis to solve this problem, ad hoc associations, committees, commissions, and authorities have been formed, which amounts to the proverbial equivalent of bringing a pocket knife to a gun fight.

Take, for example, the Nile Basin, a crucial area of the continent that encompasses 11 states with a total population of more than 430 million people. For decades, people is this area have been suffering from severe food shortages and chronic poverty, tied directly to the critical shortage of irrigated farming.[58] To address these problems, and to manage the water-related resources of the Nile River, an ineffective ad hoc association has been created which, to date, has failed to produce any tangible results.[59] The Nile Basin Initiative (NBI), formed by ten

Nile Basin states over 20 years ago, is one, among many, intergovern-mental partnerships specifically designed to address the agricultural and biodiversity problems facing the region. Its specific mission has been 'To take care of and jointly use the shared Nile Basin water and related resources.' Not only has this not happened, the furor that has been brewing between Egypt and Ethiopia—over the latter's decision to move forward with the Grand Ethiopian Renaissance Dam—belies any success the NBI would like to claim.[60]

The problems surrounding the Niger River Basin—Africa's third largest river body, surrounded by nine West African States, with a population of over 150 million people—produced, years earlier, the same ad hoc intergovernmental response. As the precursor to the NBI, the Niger Basin Authority (NBA), formed nearly 50 years ago, began with a very similar mission: 'To improve the living conditions of the basin populations through sustainable management of water resources and associated ecosystems.'[61] However, for reasons that inhibit the NBI from achieving any meaningful results, most notably inadequate funding and the absence of centralized political authority, the efforts of the NBA, and many other organizations of this sort, have been for naught. This explains why African farmers throughout the continent are still obliged to pray to the rain gods each year for help with their rain-dependent farms.

There are 63 transboundary river basins in Africa, not least of which include, also, the Congo, Zambezi, and Orange river basins. Moreover, these basins cover approximately 64 percent of Africa's landmass. And while there are other important factors that contribute to malnutri-tion in Africa, for example, transportation, storage, seed, fertilizer, and value-addition problems, water is life. Relatedly, it is an open secret that the Sahara Desert—the third largest desert in the world, which currently occupies approximately one-third of Africa—could be largely reclaimed and made to bloom into an agricultural oasis.[62] Bordered, directly, by 11 states in north, west, and east Africa, what better project for a Union Government of Africa than the blooming of the Sahara Desert?

Finally, independent of the critical need to irrigate the continent which, again, is a continent-wide task, it is also important to appreciate the huge amount of cultivable land in Africa, approximately 632 million hectares.[63] This arable land, nearly 80 percent of which lays agriculturally dormant, is capable of feeding billions of people, both inside and outside Africa. Unfortunately, much of this arable land, that which is cultivated and that which is not, suffers from various forms of degradation due, pri-marily, to extensive farming, deforestation, and overgrazing. Moreover, the severe shortage of investment resources, electricity, and technological expertise further hinders Africa from realizing its agricultural potential. In fact, the DRC, alone, has the agricultural potential to feed the entire African continent![64] This is the same Congo—thanks to the Congo River Basin—that has the hydroelectric capacity to electrify 60 percent of the entire continent with more than 150,000 megawatts of power. However, what the DRC lacks is what Africa lacks, the convergence of investment resources and policy planning from a Union Government of Africa, devoid of the interference, arm-twisting, myopia, and financial strangulation of the IMF, WB, EU, the United States, China, and other so-called partner nations and institutions.

Industry

The argument for the necessity of adding value to African raw materials and mineral resources, *in Africa*, has been won, decades ago, and needs no further discussion. It is clearly one of the cornerstones of any plan to industrialize Africa. Relatedly, there is no better way of eliminating Africa's current $35 billion food bill—estimated by some to reach $110 billion by 2025[65]—than by merging food crop production with industry. Failure to recognize and act upon these two axioms of industrial development will amount to (1) frequent malnutrition, especially in light of the harmful impact climate change is having on African agrarian yields; (2) continued exportation of millions of jobs abroad, at the expense of mounting unemployment in Africa; and (3) heightened external debt, causing budget crippling, balance of payments crises throughout the continent.

The most pressing question today, then, remains the same as it was since independence: How best to implement these eternal truths of industrial development? As Nkrumah outlined years ago, and expressed below, continental planning, not ad hoc associations, will only do.

> It is quite obvious that integrated continental planning cannot find a substitute in the kind of tinkering that limits us to inter-territorial associations within customs unions, trade agreements, inter-communications services, and the like. While these will naturally increase our common intercourse and provide for certain inter-action, they can only be partially beneficial in their effects. For such tinkering does not create the decisive conditions for resolute development, since it ignores the crucial requirement of continental integration as the essential prerequisite for the most bountiful economic progress, which must be based in the widest possible extension of land and population.[66]

Along these lines, continent-wide geological, geographical, and demographic surveying will enable us to know what are the best natural resources and agricultural crops to produce, and where are the best locations in Africa to produce them.[67] These questions can only be answered after a continent-wide assessment of Africa is made regarding (1) the environmental advantages of the mineral deposits, soil quality, water bodies, and climate variation of the different geographical regions; (2) the demographical advantages of labour availability, market size, and economies of scale; and (3) the feasibility of transportation access and expansion in order to facilitate regional and/ or continent-wide distribution. We all like to eat chocolate and drink tea, but can we and, more importantly, should we try producing these items in Africa, willy-nilly, without careful, scientific planning? The same question could be raised regarding paper, rubber, and cloth— each of which we actually need. Paper mills, rubber plantations, and textile factories have ideal environments to operate based on some of the factors of production noted above. In short, in our efforts to realize the fullest (productive) potential of the continent and its people, the geographical and economic viability of every project must be weighed, carefully, against the risk of wasteful duplication, financial loss, and environmental damage.

The production of iron and steel, derivatives of iron ore, will also have to be given top priority: these two substances are indispensable in the industrial development of any nation. So, too, obviously, are energy resources. Here, again, continental surveying will enable us to know where the high quality ores are located in Africa, especially those worthy of the huge investment required to unearth them from the ground. Planned continental surveying will also enable us to know where Africa's abundant renewable energy resources (of sunlight, natural gas, wind, tides, waves, hydropower, and others) are located. And in order to reduce the expense of electricity *transmission*, it would only be logical to build the huge iron and steel production complexes that are needed, in relatively close proximity to where energy is *generated*. This steel, then, can be distributed throughout the continent for the production of automobiles, trains, planes, ships, iron rods, bicycles and, in addition to thousands of other steel derived products, the mass production of various types of farm machinery needed in the mechanization of agriculture (the arrival of drone technology notwithstanding). In each and every case, along the way, planning must always (1) take into account Africa's concrete conditions and unique circumstances as noted above; (2) be driven by the aim of developing clusters of industrial growth poles in every region of Africa; and (3) fall under the guidance and centralized authority of a Union Government of Africa committed to the industrial development of the continent.

Health

The 2014–2016 Ebola outbreak in West Africa was a watershed moment in the ongoing health crisis facing the African continent.[68] With the death toll having reached 11,310, it underscored a number of critical problems that only continent-wide planning can solve: (1) lack of cross-border collaboration in prevention, preparedness, and contingency of disease control; (2) lack of (timely and accurate) information sharing and exchange in order to reduce the risks of transmission of infectious disease-causing pathogens; and (3) lack of financial resources for investment in the health sector, especially public health, including indigenous led pharmaceutical research devoted to those diseases that most affect Africa. Unfortunately, to date, only ad hoc solutions have been proposed, as in the ten-country, *unfunded*, response to the most recent, and second largest, Ebola outbreak in the world in the DRC.[69] Without a continental Pan-African approach, the 'free flow of goods, services, and people,' to which all advocates of African integration and unity subscribe, will never be properly realized.

In addition to the challenges posed by pandemics, including COVID-19, the broader areas of Africa's health crisis, including all manner of other infectious and chronic diseases, can only be addressed by a Union Government of Africa committed to the *socialist* principle of universal health coverage for every citizen of Africa.[70] This will require a hefty investment in public health, with an emphasis in preventive care, and a proper management of Africa's healthcare resources, both human and physical. External support from special grants and funds of various humanitarian projects will always be welcomed. However, the abundance of wealth and human resources available to a Union Government of Africa, when managed efficiently, will be more than enough to meet the health challenges of the African nation.

Biodiversity

The urgent need for continental planning can never be better understood than by examining the severe vulnerability of Africa's biodiversity. This is because the colossal damage being done to human life and the physical environment in Africa shows absolutely no regards for the continent's colonial derived borders. We can begin with the rising sea levels along much of the West African coastline, from Mauritania to Cameroon, where thousands of communities are at risk of being washed away.[71] Tragically, Africa's northeastern coastline, from Egypt to Mozambique, has not been spared either. Driven largely by global warming, the ultimate impact this climatic onslaught could have on these coastal centres of commerce, trade, industry, fisheries, tourism, and residential expansion is overwhelming.[72] However, as alarming as these future projections are, it is the recent past and the current situation which are most troublesome for the 39 states in Africa that are either bordered or surrounded by the sea. Among the most destructive effects, the following are worthy of note: (1) salinization, that is, the increasing concentration of the ocean's salt into African soils used for farming; (2) flooding of coastal villages, towns, and cities which impact a wide spectrum of economic activities, resulting in a significantly lowered GDP and the forced migration of millions of people; and (3) pollution of aquifers, that is, the loss of invaluable habitats for fish, birds, and plants.

Sadly, once again, only ad hoc solutions have been proposed to solve these disastrous problems, problems that effect nearly two-thirds of the continent, directly, and the remaining portion, indirectly. The Gulf of Guinea Commission, comprised of seven countries, is one such grouping.[73] Formed in 2001, this vastly underfunded institution is guilty of biting off far more than it can chew. Besides aiming to protect the region's incredible biodiversity, a singularly Herculean task in itself, other critically important objectives contained within its mandate include (1) maintaining maritime peace, (2) battling coastal piracy, (3) exploiting mineral resources, and (4) preventing illegal and unregulated fishing. In the latter case, where West Africa, alone, loses more than 40 percent of its fish, annually, to illegal fishing perpetrated by foreign vessels from Europe and Asia,[74] nothing less than a Union African Government response will do. At an annual loss of $1.3 billion, this illegal and unregulated activity, nay, international crime, destroys marine habitats, inhibits the renewability of invaluable fishing stocks, and denies employment for millions of people who depend on fishing for their livelihood. Regional ad hoc associations, devoid of any government centralized (and military) authority, will only drown under such heavy responsibility. This is all the more true when you consider that Africa's other coastal communities lying on the Mediterranean and Indian oceans face an identical plight.[75]

The challenges facing Africa's *inland* biodiversity are no less severe. The activities causing this damage, resulting primarily from Africa's neo-colonized status, are both legal and illegal. The catastrophic loss of Africa's rain forest, for example, amounts to the destruction of over four million hectares of forest cover every year. This is twice the global defor-estation rate! And once again, this alarming reality, as with all the others, shows no respect for Africa's artificial boundaries: It causes soil erosion and rain scarcity in huge (cross-boundary) tracts of once fertile land.[76] In addition to these nefarious logging practices, both legal and illegal, the contribution mining operations are making to the destruction of Africa's inland (borderless) biodiversity are no less significant.[77] Take small-scale gold mining, for example, as practiced in different parts of Africa. Its use of mercury, the cheapest and simplest way to extract gold from soil and sedimentary rocks, is poisoning large river bodies that, in their retreat to the sea, flow (with turbid toxicity) across borders in several countries before reaching their final destination. The yellowish brown, lethal mess Ghana has made of the Bia and Tano rivers, both of which flow into the territory of their western neighbour, La Cote d'Ivoire, serves as a vivid illustration of the Pan-African dimensions of this calamity.[78]

Human life and entire ecosystems across the continent are either at considerable risk or are suffering ineffable damage from a wide range of environmental despoilers. Most recently, the deadly locust infest-ation, another consequence of climate change, is devastating crops and pastures in at least nine countries in northeast and central Africa. This is effecting the food security of over 360 million people, nearly one-third of the entire population of Africa. Yet, in the absence of continent-wide planning, buttressed by the legislation, regulation, and funding of a Union Government of Africa, we are left with the futile strategy of reacting, ineffectively, to one environmental crisis after another with ad hoc committees and associations.

Ocean access

Approximately 30 per cent of African countries are landlocked without immediate access to the sea. The consequences of this predicament for those affected countries are serious and serve as major impediments to their potential for full-scale economic development. In this regard, it is not by mere happenstance that many landlocked countries are among some of the poorest countries in the world. In short, having immediate access to the sea offers a wide range of economic and political benefits to those counties with borders lying on the ocean;[79] conversely, being without immediate access to the sea creates huge challenges for non-coastal nations.[80] The reasons for this are fairly obvious: with oceans covering 71 percent of the surface of the earth, their depth containing 300 times the habitable volume of terrestrial habitats on the earth, the far majority of what we know as life on earth exists in the oceans.

Imagine, then, what this means for so-called developing countries that are landlocked. They would, in effect, lack access to fish and abundant oceanic food sources; lack access to raw materials, mineral resources, and medicinal florae, all found, in abundance, under the sea; face expensive transportation costs to collect and send goods, because of not having access to ports and international shipping operations which, in turn, severely hampers their trading potential and global market access; be cut off from humongous recreational and tourism revenue, the leading source of foreign exchange—read: financial life-blood—for many countries with immediate access to the sea; and, finally, be made subject to the geopolitical interests and military advantages of their neighbours and other nations with direct naval opportunities.[81] This, still, is another reason why Africa must unite! It will not only provide the benefits and opportunities, mentioned above, for the effected regions in Africa. A united Africa will also significantly reduce the tensions and conflicts between African states and their peoples, many of whom, prior to the artificially drawn boundaries of the continent, had, in fact, immediate access to the sea. A Union Government of Africa will provide all of its people—including those living in the 17 landlocked states—with the enormous benefits of being citizens of a nation that has immediate access to the sea on every corner of its borders.

Conflict resolution and military defence

The balkanization of Africa, consecrated at the infamous Berlin Conference of 1884–1885, not only created small, economically nonviable dependencies in Africa; it also engendered and exacerbated ethnic and religious hostilities throughout the continent. This longstanding strategy of 'divide and rule' was used to perfection throughout much of Africa, which now has more borders—well over a 100—than any other continent on earth. The recipe was simple: fossilize Africa's various ethnic groups, many of whom were historical rivals, then force them under one geopolitical roof with preferences given, in some instances, to one group over another. Independence, then, would be fraught with so many ethnic (and religious) hostilities and antagonisms that national integration and political stability, prerequisites for economic develop-ment, would be practically impossible.[82] As a result, we have a continent replete with intrastate and interstate conflicts, many of which, over the years, have blossomed into full-scale civil wars.

Consequently, only the full-scale might of an All-African Military High Command, under the centralized authority of a Union Government of Africa, will be able to solve these incessant conflicts and end these devastating wars, including the various forms of violence resulting from both Christian and Islamic extremism. The UN, NATO, EU, the United States, or any other entity outside of Africa can never, and will never, solve our internal problems. None of them have the genuine interest, will, means, or mandate to do so. Instead, if left in the hands of outside forces, many of whom operate with agendas contrary to the aims of a liberated Africa, they are more likely, as they have demonstrated repeatedly, of making matters worse. This results in an Africa more malleable than ever for continued imperialist domination.[83] Who, after all, manoeuvred the great Pan-Africanist, Patrice Lumumba, out of office in the Congo and into the murderous clutches of the CIA, the Belgians, and their puppet soldier, Mobutu Sese Seku?[84] Who pulled their troops out of Rwanda and failed to protect the lives of over 800,000 victims of genocide?[85] And who orchestrated and sponsored the civil war in Libya that resulted in the assassination of Muamar Gaddafi, one of Africa's most veritable Pan-Africanists?[86] The list could go on and on, including, more recently, the inability of the UN to prevent war-torn southeast DRC from becoming the 'Rape Capital of the World.'[87] Is there any wonder, then, why UN 'Peacekeepers' in Mozambique, Guinea, Sierra Leone, Liberia, and Haiti have been found guilty of fathering hundreds of children with local women and girls, in some cases subjecting them to the most virulent forms of sexual violence and exploitation?[88]

However, as quiet as it has been kept, Africa, itself, has an outstanding record of resolving its own conflicts, and it has done so from times immemorial.[89] Throughout the continent, there were many traditional systems and institutions, strikingly similarity to each other, that were designed to resolve inter and intra ethnic and regional conflicts long before the European encroachment of Africa.[90] Unfortunately, as with many indigenous African cultural patterns, these arbitration customs were either jettisoned or marginalized in favour of Eurocentric models of operation.

Nonetheless, the tools for ending conflicts and building peace throughout Africa still lies essentially *in* Africa *among* Africans. More recently, this has been evidenced by the indispensable role played by African women in helping to resolve conflicts and build peace throughout the continent.[91] Indeed, their success record, especially in countries like Liberia and Sierra Leone in West Africa, and Rwanda in East Africa, has been far better than the intervention experiences and mediating efforts of some of the regional (male dominated) ad hoc military formations.[92] In this regard, the Economic Community of West African States Monitoring Group (ECOMOG) readily comes to mind. A weak resolve, inadequate funding, poor planning, flawed logistics, and uncertain objectives—all of which could have been remedied with an All-African Military High command—were the main factors that contributed to the blunders ECOMOG made in West Africa.[93] Unfortunately, much of these same criticisms can be levelled at the AU's Standby Force (ASF), which has been plagued by poorly trained soldiers, ill-equipped armies, underfunded operations, and lack of centralized control.[94] And although the AFS and the various regional ad hoc groupings have not experienced complete failure, clearly the primary victims of war and conflict in Africa, women (and children), need to be at the forefront of any attempt to end conflicts and build peace in Africa. Who has a greater reason for this to happen than African women, whose lives have been ruined by ethnic conflicts, tribal wars, political violence, and (even) the sexual exploitation by African peacekeeping soldiers? And who is better equipped to make this happen than African women, who find it much easier than men to cross the explosive boundaries of religion, ethnicity, and party affiliation? Their socialization, alone, along with their vested interest in peace, renders them the greatest stakeholders for peace that we have. A Bureau of Women Affairs, then, as an integral part of a Union Government of Africa, must be charged with the responsibility of institutionalizing a pivotal role for women in conflict resolution and peace building in Africa. With proper training, a steadfast commitment to Pan-Africanism, and the backing of a Union Government of Africa, African women, especially women from the grassroots, could be deployed throughout the continent, alongside their male counterparts, as Africa's primary arbitrators, negotiators, conciliators, and mediators.

On the international front, an effective defence against foreign espionage and aggression has to be one of the top priorities on the African development agenda. Without it, whatever gains we have made towards a unified and socialist Africa will remain in mortal danger of being completely dismantled. Who begrudges China for acquiring the military capacity to protect the Chinese homeland, including building an arsenal of inter-continental ballistic missiles capable of reaching anywhere in the world in a matter of minutes? Had they not, how safe, how secure, would their standing be as a growing industrial giant and formidable global power? Global peace, *with justice*, including universal nuclear disarmament, has to be the ultimate objective of all peoples around the world. However, until we get there, nay, *in order to get there*, Africa will have to be in a position to repel or dissuade any other country, or groups of countries, from (1) establishing military bases on its shores, (2) using its arm forces to fight proxy wars in pursuit of foreign interests, and

(3) bullying it into economic and political submission. This can only be achieved by the power derived from a Union Government of Africa.

In its absence, a balkanized Africa will have the billions of dollars it spends on military hardware, and millions of its uniformed soldiers stretched across the continent, dissipated into ineffectiveness—the existence of regional ad hoc military groups and the ASF notwithstanding. Into this void slips NATO, EU, and single country interlopers, each geared to maintaining geopolitical dominance in Africa while protecting the financial interests of the Global North (*vis a vis* its adversaries, e.g., China, Russia, and others). While France has become a perfectionist in this regard,[95] one of the more recent and most troubling examples of this, because of its continental reach, is the United States African Command (AFRICOM).[96] With very little transparency, AFRICOM has undertaken thousands of military missions in Africa since its inception in 2008, including a growing number of airstrikes. This has been carried out with thousands of US troops, weaponized drone bases, and the connivance of various African governments scattered across the continent. Only a Union Government of Africa will be able to put an end to foreign interference and establish an effective military defence of the African motherland from internal and external threats. This must include conducting its own intelligence gatherings, surveillance operations, and reconnaissance missions. What is at stake is the peace and prosperity that Africa so urgently needs.

Asserting the African personality

It is long overdue for Africa to assert, as a sovereign nation, its own unique view of the world. This view, which Nkrumah conceptualized as the African Personality,[97] should be expressed with an unwavering conviction. Moreover, it should be regarded and respected by the rest of the world, especially where it really matters: within the various corridors of global power. The world, after all, has much to learn from Africa! Holding a seat on the Security Council of the United Nations, for instance, should be one of the primary pursuits of a Union Government of Africa. What better way to insert its world view into the global arena than by sitting down with other nations, as equals, and discussing, through deliberation and debate, the important matters impacting the global community?

Such a view assumes not only a shared common history (and destiny), but also a shared common cultural heritage as well. In the former case, it would not be difficult to argue that, historically, no region in Africa has been unaffected, directly or indirectly, by the relentless onslaught of intruders, invaders, occupiers, enslavers, and colonizers, in short, predator nations from Asia and Europe who entered Africa's shores and caused havoc throughout the continent. Collectively, they have rendered Africa into a state of political and economic prostration.[98] This centuries-old experience, alone, has left socio-economic and political scars that are still evident today and serve as a critical part of the African World view. The African Personality, then, includes a shared understanding of this history, a history which encompasses the experiences of Africans at home and abroad. However, it is important to note that this shared history is not just a history of foreign domination. It is also a history that encompasses the various phases of African development, from the African origins of human civilization to the evolution and vicissitudes of building empires and nation-states throughout the continent. It also includes the liberation struggles in Africa and its diaspora against various forms of oppression, exploitation, and degradation.

The other main component of the African Personality, a common cultural heritage, is also shared by countless millions of Africans at home and abroad. This is not to suggest there is no cultural diversity *in* Africa and *among* Africans, globally. Quite the contrary, nor would that be a favourable situation even if it were true. Indeed, the diversity of cultural practices found amongst the African people provides Africa with an invaluable resource—a bank of kaleidoscopic cultural patterns that reflects its people's successful struggle to adapt, survive, and (frequently) flourish in the various environs they have found themselves over the centuries. However, it is also clear that there are a number of commonly shared cultural patterns, even whole institutions, that can be found in African communities throughout the world, and for which Africans are best known. The reason for this is simple: From times immemorial, that is, centuries before the foreign encroachments, Africans had been interacting, exchanging, and engaging with each other across wide geographical axes of the continent—from the Nile Valley to the Congo Basin, from Senegal to Niger, from the Congo to the Zambesi, from South Africa to Angola, and from everywhere else in between. And given the indelible nature of cultural creations, it is no wonder that Africans share so many fundamentally similar cultural patterns, in *essence*, even if they appear, on the surface, to be different in *form*. The obvious ones include family structure, religious worship, political governance, and the arts, including both visual and performance. The less obvious ones, yet no less significant, include the more ethereal concepts of space, time, and being. Africans forcibly removed to the Americas during the trans-Atlantic slave era, and their descendants, would not have been able to adapt, survive, and (frequently) flourish in the hostile environs they were taken to without the use of these indigenous cultural patterns.[99]

Finally, it would be remiss to not also recognize the significant role Euro-Christianity and Arab-Islam have played in shaping the African Personality. Indeed, as Nkrumah warned years ago, it is critical that these two experiences, both important in Africa's evolution, be digested and assimilated into the tapestry of African cultural patterns in such a way as to ensure peace and harmony while elevating Africa's humanist and egalitarian past.[100] In this way, the African Personality becomes both inclusive and dynamic, and, as Nkrumah has argued, '… finds expression in a re-awakening consciousness among Africans and peoples of African descent of the bonds which unite us—our historical past, our culture, our common experience, and our aspirations.'[101] In sum, Africa's ability to impact the world with its own particular points of view and frames of reference on the critical matters of the day—for example, on migration, climate change, nuclear disarmament, world hunger, child labour, sex trafficking, global viral infections, and countless others—will only be realized when a Union Government of Africa is built and fully functioning. On the African Personality, we give Nkrumah the final words:

> It is a concept of the African nation, and is not associated with a particular state, language, religion, political system, or colour of the skin. For those who project it, it expresses identification not only with Africa's historical past, but with the struggle of the African people in the African Revolution to liberate and unify the continent and to build a just society.[102]

To assert the African Personality in the world, and for it to be genuinely felt, Africa must unite.

Conclusion

As can be surmised from the discussion above, the type of unification required to ensure the complete and rapid development of the continent cannot be achieved within the institutional confines of the AU, its various branches, networks and programs, and the regional ad hoc associations it endorses. This is due largely to the lack of proper funding and the absence of centralized authority, two of the most important prerequisites to ensuring institutional success, both of which are severely hampering the operations of the AU and its affiliates. With funding, regrettably, the AU relies on foreign donations for nearly two-thirds of its budgetary needs, with more than 40 percent of its member states not paying their annual dues (of 0.2 percent levy on eligible imports).[103] Even more regrettable, bordering on the deplorable, African Heads of State allowed the Chinese government—a government which prides itself on self-reliance—to finance and construct the AU Headquarters in Addis Ababa at the whopping cost of $200 million.[104] This bizarre dispensation merely served as the prelude to the AU's consistent dependency on foreign donations from Canada, Sweden, Germany, the Netherlands, the United States, the UK, China, the WB, and the EU over the past 20 years of its existence. Sadly, just recently, the EU has decided that it will no longer follow the guidance of the AU in determining how EU funding for 'Peace and Security' will be used in conflict prevention and resolution in Africa.[105] What exemplifies the impotence of the AU more than Europe's highest governing body, the EU, providing military support in Africa for whichever military factions it deems appropriate without any regards for the concerns and interests of Africa's highest governing body, the AU?

The absence of centralized authority guiding the various programs and projects of the AU and its affiliate institutions, which reduces their operations to little more than volunteerism, is no less critical than the lack of funding. The AU's schizophrenic Constitutive Act, especially in Article 4, does not help: Member States are obliged to follow both the principle of 'non-interference in the internal affairs of other states' *and* the principle of 'having the right of the AU to intervene in a Member State in respect of grave circumstances.'[106] And no matter how grave the circumstances are, 'including war crimes, genocide and crimes against humanity,' a Member State can merely voluntarily withdraw from the AU to prevent it from being intervened by the AU. As a result, for the past 20 years the AU's record in resolving conflicts and building peace in Africa has been lacklustre, at best, exemplified most blatantly in its inability to protect the life of Muamar Gaddafi and preventing Libya from descending into a violent ethnic morass. Its inability of preventing the ethnic carnage and accompanying sexual violations in Ethiopia is yet, still, another more recent example.

This same absence of centralized authority, coupled with the absence of continental strategic planning, may soon doom the new AfCFTA to a similar fate, especially if there is no Union Government pursuing socialist policies. As it stands now, private companies of Member States are all gearing up to compete against their rivals in other Member States for a slice of the fiercely expanding African market. As with any market-driven capitalist economy, some giant and semi-giant companies, especially in some of the larger Member States, may *win* and gain a greater share of the African market. However, the *losers*, as discussed in Chapter 4, will be far greater. Furthermore, the elimination of tariff barriers throughout Africa, the *raison d'être* of the AfCFTA, represents only a small portion of the problems inhibiting intra-African trade. The other critically important elements—for example, pitiable interstate road infrastructure, staggering currency transaction costs, and complex immigration procedures, to name but a few—can only be addressed with the power derived from continental unification. And finally, the AfCFTA will play absolutely no role in regaining the control international finance capital has over Africa's mineral resources and raw materials. Only a Union Government of Africa can achieve this monumental objective.

Notes

1 Kwame Nkrumah, *Revolutionary Path*, New York: International, 1973, pg. 183.
2 Ukertor Gabriel Moti, 'Africa's Natural Resource Wealth: A Paradox of Plenty and Poverty,' *Advances in Social Sciences Research Journal*, Vol. 6, No. 7, July 25, 2019, pgs. 483–504.
3 Chancellor Williams, *The Destruction of Black Civilization: Great Issues of a Race, 4500 BC to 2000 AD*, Chicago: Third World, 1987, Chapter. VIII.
4 Ibid.
5 David Newbury, 'Pre-Colonial Burundi and Rwanda: Local Loyalties, Regional Loyalties,' *The International Journal of African Historical Studies*, Vol. 34, No. 2, 2001, pgs. 255–314.
6 Laurel L. Rose, 'African Elite's Land Control Maneuvers,' *Etudes Rurales*, 2002, Vol. 163–164, pgs. 187–213; Kwame Nkrumah, *Class Struggle in Africa*, New York: International, 1970; Ikechi Mgbeoji, 'The Comprador Complex: Africa's IPRs Elite, Neo-colonialism and the Enduring Control of African IPRs Agenda by External Interests,' *Osgoode Legal Studies Research Paper No. 32*, Vol. 10, No. 8, 2014; Hazel M. McFerson, 'Governance and Hyper-corruption in Resource-rich African Countries,' *Third World Quarterly*, Vol. 30, No. 8, 2009, pgs. 1529–1548.
7 George J. Coakley and Philip M. Mobbs, *The Mineral Industries of Africa*, https://minerals.usgs.gov/minerals/pubs/country/1999/africa99.pdf, 1999; A. Williams Postel, *The Mineral Resources of Africa*, Philadelphia: University of Pennsylvania Press, 1943.
8 Conflicts in Africa around oil and gas.
9 Tendai Murisa, *Africa: The Billions that Got Away*. Trust Africa. Mail & Guardian Africa, www.tralac.org/images/docs/7771/africa-the-billions-that-got-away-mg-2015.pdf; African Development Bank and Global Financial Integrity, *Illicit Financial Flows and the Problem of Net Resource Transfers from Africa: 1980–2009*. Washington, DC: Global Financial Integrity, May 2013.

10 Manitra A. Rakotoarisoa et al., *Why Has Africa Become a Net Food Importer: Explaining Africa Agricultural and Food Trade Deficits*, Rome: FAO, UN, 2012.

11 C. Jean Arment, 'Food Dependency in Sub-Saharan Africa: Simply a Matter of "Vulnerability" or, Missed Development Opportunity?', *Development and Change: Forum 2020*, March 2020, Vol. 51, No. 2, pgs. 283–323; Manitra A. Rakotoarisoa et al., *Why Has Africa Become a Net Importer of Food? Explaining Africa Agricultural and Food Trade Deficits*, Trade and Markets Division FAO, 2011.

12 Roger Blein et al., *Agriculture in Africa: Transformation and Outlook*, Johannesburg: NEPAD, 2013.

13 Altchenko, Yvan and Villholth, Karen G., 'Mapping Irrigation Potential from Renewable Groundwater in Africa – A Quantitative Hydrological Approach,' *Hydrology and Earth System Sciences Discussions*, Vol. 11, No. 6, pgs. 6065–6097, 2014; Pavelic, Paul et al., 'Identifying the Barriers and Pathways Forward for Expanding the use of Groundwater for irrigation in Sub-Saharan Africa,' *Water International*, Vol. 38, No. 4, pgs. 363–368, 2013; Gebregziabher, Gebrehaweria, et al., 'Cost-benefit analysis and ideas for cost sharing of groundwater irrigation: evidence from north-eastern Ethiopia, *Water International*, Vol. 38, No. 6, pgs. 852–863, 2013.

14 Wojciechowska-Shibuya, Marisha, Ed., Unlocking Africa's Transboundary Water Potential, African Development Bank, 2016.

15 This very commitment was made in a declaration approved by the African Heads of State at the African Union Summit on Water and Sanitation held in Sharm El-Sheikh, Egypt in June–July 2008. See Alison Dittmer, *Sharm El-Sheikh and Water Aid: Turning Commitment into Action*, London: Water Aid, 2009; Investing in greywater system management should also be a part of Africa's future planning in water system management, Fulvio Boano et al., 'A Review of Nature-Based Solutions for Greywater Treatment: Applications, Hydraulic Design, and Environmental Benefits, *Science for the Total Environment*, Vol. 711, April 1, 2020, retrieved from: https://doi.org/10.1016/j.scitotenv.2019.134731.

16 Emanuel Achor, 'Energy Crisis and Sustainable Development in Africa: Perspectives of Some Nigerians on Awareness, Causes, and Way Forward,' *OIDA International Journal of Sustainable Development*, January 2012, Vol. 2, No. 20; Justice Tei Mensah, 'Jobs! Electricity Shortages and Unemployment in Africa,' Policy Research Paper 8415, World Bank Group, African Region Office of Chief Economist, April 2018, Retrieved from: http://documents1.worldbank.org/curated/en/659751524142624281/pdf/Jobs-electricity-shortages-and-unemployment-in-Africa.pdf; Africa Energy Outlook 2019, World Energy Outlook Special Report, Country Report—November 2019, Retrieved from: www.iea.org/reports/africa-energy-outlook-2019.

17 Paul Collier et al., 'Climate Change and Africa, *Oxford Review of Economic Policy*, Vol. 24, No. 2, Summer 2008, pgs. 337–353; Scott Fields, 'Continental Divide: Why Africa's Climate Change Burden is Greater,' *Environmental Health Perspectives*, August 2005, pgs. A534–A537.

18 IRENA, Scaling Up Renewable Energy Deployment in Africa, International Renewable Energy Agency, January 2019, retrieved from: www.irena.org/-/media/Files/IRENA/Agency/Regional-Group/Africa/IRENA_Africa_ impact_2019.pdf?la=en&hash=EECD0F6E8195698842965E63841284997 097D9AA; Priscillia Andrieu, 'Enchancing a Continental Policy on Energy Access in Africa, *Policy Brief*, October 2016, GMF, OCP Policy Center, retrieved from: www.irena.org/-/media/Files/IRENA/Agency/Regional-Group/Africa/IRENA_Africa_impact_2019.pdf?la=en&hash=EECD0F6 E8195698842965E63841284997097D9AA.

19 Ange Asanzi, 'The Grand Inga – A False Solution to Energy Poverty,' *African Coalition for Corporate Accountability (ACCA): Working Together to Protect Human Rights*, December 9, 2016, retrieved from: www.acca humanrights.org/en/news/member-news/144-the-grand-inga-%E2%80% 93-a-false-solution-to-energy-poverty

20 Kwame Nkrumah, *Axioms of Kwame Nkrumah: Freedom Fighter's Edition*, London: Panaf, 1967, pg. 107.

21 Hans Groth and John F. May, eds., *Africa's Population: In Search of a Demographic Dividend*, Springer, 2017.

22 'Too Many Africans?,' Stephen Corry, *Counterpunch*, July 11, 2019, www. counterpunch.org/2019/07/11/too-many-africans/.

23 See Vincent Bakpetu Thompson, *The Making of the African Diaspora in the Americas: 1441–1900*, New York, 1987 for an excellent historical account of one segment of the African Diaspora: the community of African descendants who were forced out of Africa due to the trans-Atlantic slave trade.

24 '*Meet the Ghanaian Scientist who Built InSight, NASA's Latest Spacecraft to Land on Mars.*' www.ghanaweb.com. November 29, 2018.

25 Todd Combs, 'The Remittance Sector and Diaspora Engagement in Sub-Saharan Africa: Aiding Social Development?' *Nkrumaist Review: Pan-African Perspectives on African Affairs*, Vol. 6, No. 1, August 2014, pgs. 2–13.

26 Jay Beson, 'How Bonds Aimed at the Diaspora Can Raise Crucial Funds for Africa,' *African Arguments*, July 10, 2019, https://africanarguments. org/2019/07/10/how-bonds-aimed-at-the-diaspora-can-raise-crucial-funds-for-africa/; J.K. Kwakye, *Overcoming Africa's Addiction to Foreign Aid: A Look at Some Financial Engineering to Mobilize Other Sources*, Institute of Economic Affairs, No. 32 IEA Monograph, 2010, pgs. 18–19.

27 Trevor Hambayi, 'Africa's Ticking Time Bond: $35 Billion Worth of Eurobond Debt,' *The Conversation*, May 19, 2016, https://theconversation. com/africas-ticking-time-bomb-35-billion-worth-of-eurobond-debt-59404; Misheck Mutize, 'Eurobonded: African Countries Aren't Borrowing Too Much—They're Paying Too Much for Debt,' *Quartz Africa*, February 22, 2020, https://qz.com/africa/1806793/imf-world-bank-are-wrong-africa-is-piling-on-too-much-debt/.

28 Kevin K. Gaines, *American Africans in Ghana: Black Expatriates and the Civil Rights Era*, Chapel Hill: University of North Carolina Press, 2006.

29 Kwame Nkrumah, *Class Struggle in Africa*, New York: International, 1970, pg. 87.
30 Mick More et al., *Taxing Africa: Coercion, Reform, and Development*, London: Zed, 2018.
31 'Trade Misinvoicing or How to Steal from Africa,' Brian LeBlanc, May 6, 2014, Global Financial Integrity: https://gfintegrity.org/press-release/trade-misinvoicing-or-how-to-steal-from-africa/; https://thinkafricapress.com/trade-misinvoicing-how-to-steal-from-africa/.
32 Sweet Nothings: The Human Cost of a British Sugar Giant Avoiding Taxes in Southern Africa, Action Aid, https://actionaid.org/sites/default/files/swe et_nothings.pdf, February 10, 2013.
33 Benoit Blarel et al., eds., *Illegal Logging, Fishing, and Wildlife Trade: The Costs and How to Combat It*, World Bank Group, October 2019, retrieved from: http://pubdocs.worldbank.org/en/482771571323560234/WBGRe port1017Digital.pdf; Christian Nellemann, eds., *Illegal Logging, The Environmental Crime Crisis: Threats to Sustainable Development From Illegal Exploitation and Trade in Wildlife and Forests Resources*, UNEP – INTERPOL, 2014.
34 Stephanie Bouckaert et al., *Africa Energy Outlook 2019, World Energy Outlook Special Report*, International Energy Agency (IEA), November 2019, pgs. 41–44; Kevin Watkins et al., *Power, People, Planet: Seizing Africa's Energy and Climate Opportunities*, Africa Progress Report 2015, pg. 17, retrieved from: https://reliefweb.int/sites/reliefweb.int/files/resources/ APP_REPORT_2015_FINAL_low1.pdf
35 Stephanie Bouckaert, ibid.; EIA, *Energy Implications of Higher Economic Growth in Africa*, U.S. Energy Information Administration, 2018, retrieved from: www.tralac.org/documents/news/2100-ieo2018-energy-implications-of-higher-economic-growth-in-africa-eia-july-2018/file.html.
36 'Foreign Exchange Reserves in Africa: Benefits, Costs and Political Economy Considerations,' Jochen Schanz Monetary and Economic Department of the Bank of International Settlements, Papers No. 15, October 2019.
37 Landry Signé, *Africa's Consumer Market Potential: Trends, Drivers, Opportunities, and Strategies*, Africa Growth Initiative, Brookings Institution, December 2018.
38 Food Fortification Initiative, Global Alliance for Improved Nutrition (GAIN), Enhancing Grains for Healthier Lives: Republic of Ghana, retrieved from: http://ffinetwork.org/about/stay_informed/releases/images/ Rice_Ghana.pdf; David Boansi and Rita M. Favour, 'Why the Persistent Increase in Rice in Ghana's Rice Imports? Prescriptions for Future Rice Policy,' *Asian Journal of Agricultural Extension, Economics, and Sociology*, Vol. 7, No. 4, August 2015, pgs. 1–21.
39 Manitra A. Rakotoarisoa et al., Why Has Africa Become a Net Food Importer? Explaining African Agricultural and Food Deficits, Trade and Markets Division, FAO, 2011, retrieved from: www.nielsjohannesen.net/wp-content/uploads/AJR2020-WBWP.pdf, Food Sovereignty is Africa's Only

Solution to Climate Chaos, GRAIN Report, 2019, retrieved from: https://grain.org/system/articles/pdfs/000/006/293/original/Africa%20climate%20EN%2006.pdf?1567697870.

40 Agreement Establishing the African Continental Free Trade Area, https://au.int/sites/default/files/treaties/36437-treaty-consolidated_text_on_cfta_-_en.pdf.

41 Ibid.

42 *Charter of the Organization of African Unity*, https://au.int/sites/default/files/treaties/7759-file-oau_charter_1963.pdf.

43 P. Mweti Munya, 'The Organization of African Unity and Its Role in Regional Conflict Resolution and Dispute Settlements,' *Boston College Third World Law Journal*, Vol. 19, No. 2, 1999, pgs. 537–592; Elenga M'buyinga, *Pan-Africanism or Neo-Colonialism?: The Bankruptcy of the O.A.U.*, London: Zed, 1982.

44 John, Windie, *'The Political Dynamics of Regional integration in Africa: The subjective side,'* Global Advanced Research Journal of Social Science (GARJSS) Vol. 2, No. 9, pgs. 202–211, October, 2013. Available online http://garj.org/garjss/index.htm.; Daniel Brou and Michele Ruta, 'Economic Integration, Political Integration, or Both?,' *Journal of the European Economic Association*, Vol. 9, No. 6 (December 2011), pgs. 1143–1167.

45 Larry Sawers, 'The Navigation Acts Revisited,' *Economic History Review*, Vol. XLV, No. 2, May 1992, pgs. 262–284.

46 William Hill, Protective Purpose of the Tariff Act of 1789,' *Journal of Political Economy*, Vol. 2, No. 1, December 1983, pgs. 54–76; Kevin O'Rourke, 'Tariffs and Growth in the Late 19th Century, *The Economic Journal*, Vol. 110, No. 463, April 2000, pgs. 456–483.

47 Fred Weston, The Role Played by the State in the Development of Capitalism in Japan, In Defense of Marxism, July 21, 2011, www.marxist.com/role-played-by-state-in-capitalism-in-japan.htm.

48 Yashvardhan Bardoli, 'An Ecosytem of Incentives and Policies: Economic Lessons We Can Learn from the Four Asian Tigers,' *Young Post – Discover*, November 2, 2017, www.scmp.com/yp/discover/your-voice/opinion/article/3067155/ecosystem-incentives-and-policies-economic-lessons; Dan-Bright S. Dzorgbo, 'Pathways to Economic Growth and Stagnation in Ghana: Lessons from Korea,' *Legon Journal of Sociology*, Vol. 3, No. 1, January 2006, pgs. 7–34; Jean-Germain Gros, '"Big Think," Disjointed Incrementalism: Chinese Economic Success and Policy Lessons for Africa or the Case for Pan-Africanism,' *African Journal of International Affairs*, 2008, Vol. 11, 2, No.2, pgs. 55–87.; Alvin Y. So, 'The Chinese Model of Development: Characteristics, Interpretations, Implications,' *Perspectives on Global Development and Technology*, 13 (2014), pgs. 444–464.

49 Lawrence Yaw Kusi et al., 'The Challenges and Prospects of the Commercial Poultry Industry in Ghana: A Synthesis of Literature,' *International Journal of Management Sciences*, Vol. 5, No. 6, pgs. 476–489, 2015.

50 Olu Fasan, 'Global Trade Law: Challenges and Options for Africa,' *Journal of African Law*, Vol. 47, No. 2, 2003, pgs. 143–183; Brendan Vickers, 'Africa and the Rising Powers: Bargaining for the Marginalized Many,' *Royal Institute for International Affairs*, Vol. 89, No. 3 2013, pgs. 673–693; Peter Drahos, 'When the Weak Bargain with the Strong: Negotiations in the World Trade Organization,' *International Negotiation*, Vol. 8, No. 1, pgs. 79–109, 2003.

51 Oxfam International, 'Unequal Partners: How EU-ACP Economic Partnership Agreements (EPAs) Could Harm the Development Prospects of Many of the World's Poorest Countries,' *Oxfam International Briefing Note*, September 2006; https://oxfamilibrary.openrepository.com/bitstream/han dle/10546/115057/bn-unequal-partners-epas-270906-en.pdf?sequence= 1&isAllowed=y.

52 Stephen McDonald et al., 'Why Economic Partnership Agreements Undermine Africa's Regional Integration,' *Wilson Centre and Manchester Trade Collaboration*, April 2013; www.wilsoncenter.org/sites/default/files/media/ documents/publication/EPA%20Article.pdf; Cosmas Ochieng and Tom Sharman, *Trade Traps: Why EU-ACP Economic Partnership Agreements Pose a Threat to Africa's Development*, Action Aid International, 2004, retrieved from: www.actionaid.org.uk/sites/default/files/doc_lib/trade_ traps.pdf.

53 Lord Aikins Adusei, 'Multinational Corporations: The New Colonizers in Africa,' Pambazuka News, June 4, 2009. www.pambazuka.org/governance/ multinational-corporations-new-colonisers-africa; Ilan Bijaoui, *Multinational Interest and Development in Africa: Establishing a People's Economy*, London: Palgrave McMillan, 2017.

54 Towards a Single African Currency, Proceedings of the First Congress of African Economists, March 2–4, 2019, Vol. 2, https://au.int/sites/defa ult/files/documents/31782-doc-congress_article_volume_2.pdf;   Oladele Omosegbon, 'The Significance of Common Currency to the Success of Economic Integration,' *Journal of Applied Business and Economics*, Vol. 25, No. 5, 2018, pgs. 109–119; Piotr Arak, 'Opinion: Africa does not need a single currency,' African Times, August 13, 2019 https://africatimes.com/ 2019/08/13/opinion-africa-does-not-need-a-single-currency/.

55 Peter A. Hall, 'The Euro Crisis and the Future of European Integration,' in *The Search for Europe: Contrasting Approaches*, Open Mind, BBVA, 2016, pgs. 46–67; Barry Eichengreen, 'The European Central Bank: From Problem to Solution,' ibid., pgs. 81–98.

56 Reginald H. Green and Ann Seidman, *Unity or Poverty?: The Economics of Pan-Africanism*, ibid., 232–262.

57 John Asafu-Adjaye, The Economic Impacts of Climate Change on Agriculture in Africa, *Journal of African Economies*, Vol. 23, Issue suppl_2, August 2014, Pages ii17 ii49, https://doi.org/10.1093/jae/eju 011; Robert Zougmore et al. 'Toward Climate-smart Agriculture in West

Africa: A Review of Climate Change Impacts, Adaptation Strategies and Policy Developments for the Livestock, Fishery and Crop Production Sectors,' *Agriculture & Food Security*, 2016, Vol. 5, No. 26, pgs. 1–16; David Maddison et al., 2007. The Impact of Climate Change on African Agriculture: A Ricardian Approach. Policy Research Working Paper; No. 4306. World Bank, Washington, DC. © World Bank, 2007, https://openkn owledge.worldbank.org/bitstream/handle/10986/7510/wps4306.pdf?seque nce=1&isAllowed=y.

58 John Omit et al, 'Exploration of Food Security Situation in the Nile Basin Region,' *Journal of Development and Agricultural Economics*, Vol. 3, No. 7, pgs. 274–285, August 2011.

59 Gunilla W. Olund and Ake Nilsson, 'Effectiveness of River Basin Organisations – An Institutional Review of Three African RBOs,' February 5, 2015; Alfonso Medinilla, 'African River Basin Organizations: From Best Practice to Best Fit,' *Political Economy Dynamics of Regional Organizations in Africa*, December 2018, Discussion Paper No. 236; https://ecdpm.org/ wp-content/uploads/African-river-basin-organisations-ECDPM-Discuss ion-Paper-236.pdf.

60 Ashok Swain, 'Challenges for Water Sharing in the Nile Basin Changing Geo-Politics and the Changing Climate,' Hydrological Science Journal, Vol. 56, No. 4, July 4, 2011, pgs. 687–702; Ruth Michaelson, 'It'll Cause a War: Divisions Run Deep as Filling of the Dam Nears,' *The Guardian*, April 23, 2020, www. theguardian.com/global-development/2020/apr/23/itll-cause-a-water-war-divisions-run-deep-as-filling-of-nile-dam-nears; Yahaya Ghanim, 'The Nile Basis Initiative and the Crisis of Collective Negotiations,' The Washington Institute, February 19, 2016; www.washingtoninstitute.org/policy-analysis/ view/the-nile-basin-initiative-and-the-crisis-of-collective-negotiations.

61 See: www.sath.abn.ne/; www.abn.ne/index.php?option=com_content& view= frontpage&Itemid=1&lang=en.

62 Laura Geggel, Here's How to Make the Sahara Green Again,' *Live Science*, September 12, 2018; www.livescience.com/63556-wind-solar-farms-rain-sahara-desert.html; Peter Dockrill, 'Scientists Have Announced an Incredible Plan to Make it Rain in the Sahara,' *Science Alert,* September 10, 2018, www.sciencealert.com/scientists-incredible-plan-make-rain-sahara-desert-solar-wind-energy-green-vegetation-renewable; Francesco, S.R. et al., 'The Greening of the Sahara: Past Changes and Future Implications,' One Earth, Vol. 2, No. 3, March 2020, pgs. 235–250.

63 NEPAD, *Comprehensive Africa Agricultural Programme*, November 2020, Chapter 2.2; www.fao.org/3/y6831e/y6831e00.htm#TopOfPage

64 Wim Marivoet et al., *Understanding the Democratic Republic of the Congo's Agricultural Paradox: Based on the eAtlas Platform*, International Food Policy Institute, 2018, http://ebrary.ifpri.org/utils/getfile/collection/p157 38coll2/id/132259/filename/132470.pdf.

65 Josephine Okojie, 'Africa's Food Import Bill to Reach $110bn by 2025-IITA,' *Business Day*, November 30, 2016, https://businessday.ng/agricult ure/article/africas-food-import-bill-to-reach-110bn-by-2025-iita/;   Abdur

Rahman Alfa Shaba, 'Why is Africa Importing $35bn in Food Annually,' *Africa News*, April 21, 2017, www.africanews.com/2017/04/21/why-is-africa-importing-35bn-in-food-annually-afdb-boss-asks//; *The Guardian*, 'Africa's Food Import to Hit $110 Billion by 2025,' November 7, 2018, https://guard ian.ng/business-services/africas-food-import-to-hit-110-billion-by-2025/.

66 Kwame Nkrumah, *Africa Must Unite*, New York: International, 1963, pg. 171.

67 Reginald Green and Ann Seidman, *Unity or Poverty: The Economics of Pan-Africanism*, op cit., pgs. 217–231.

68 Jean-Germain Gros, *Healthcare Policy in Africa: Institutions and Politics from Colonialism to the Present*, New York: Rowman & Littlefield, 2014, pgs. 243–261; CDC, '2014–2016 Ebola Outbreak in West Africa,' *Centers for Disease Control and Prevention*, March 8, 2019, www.cdc.gov/vhf/ebola/ history/2014-2016-outbreak/index.html.

69 WHO, 'Ten Countries Endorse Cross-Border Collaboration Framework on Ebola Outbreak Preparedness and Response,' *World Health Organization (Regional Office for Africa)*, October 21, 2019, www.afro.who.int/news/ten-african-countries-endorse-cross-border-collaboration-framework-ebola-outbreak-preparedness.

70 WHO Africa, *Universal Health Coverage for Africa: A Framework for Action*, 2016, www.afro.who.int/sites/default/files/2017-06/uhc-in-africa-a-framework-for-action.pdf.

71 Matteo Fagotto, 'Encroaching Waters Off the Coast of Togo, Ghana, Muratania, and Others are Destroying Homes, Schools, Fish, and a Way of Life,' *Foreign Policy*, October 21, 2016, https://foreignpolicy.com/2016/ 10/21/west-africa-is-being-swallowed-by-the-sea-climate-change-ghana-benin/; Sally Brown, 'African Countries Aren't Doing Enough to Prepare for Rising Sea Levels,' The Conversation, September 16, 2018, https://thec onversation.com/african-countries-arent-doing-enough-to-prepare-for-ris ing-sea-levels-103002.

72 Caleb Mensah et al., 'Assessing the Effects of Climate Change on Sea Level Rise Along the Gulf of Guinea,' *Journal of Energy and Natural Resource Management*, Vol. 4, No. 3, pgs. 15–22.

73 Treaty Establishing the Gulf of Guinea Commission, https://earth.org/sea-level-rise-west-africa-is-sinking/.

74 Nina Kaysser and Laura Adal, 'Saving Africa's Seas: The IUU Fishing Index,' *ENACT*, Issue 15, May 2020, https://enact-africa.s3.amazonaws. com/site/uploads/2020-04-06-saving-our-seas-policy-brief.pdf.

75 Ibid.

76 Hyunshik Moon and Tamirat Solomon, 'Forest Decline in Africa: Trends and Impacts of Foreign Direct Investment: A Review,' *International Journal of Current Advanced Research*, Vol. 7, No. 11, November 2018, pgs. 16356–16361; Michael Fleshman, 'Saving Africa's Forests, the "Lungs of the World,"' *African Renewal*, January 2008, www.un.org/africarenewal/ magazine/january-2008/saving-africa%E2%80%99s-forests-%E2%80% 98lungs-world%E2%80%99.

77 Flavia Olivieri, 'Artisanal and Small-Scale Mining in Africa: The Environmental and Human Costs of a Vital Livelihood Source,' *Lifegate*, November 2019, www.lifegate.com/artisanal-small-scale-mining-africa.
78 Aboka Yaw Emmanuel et al., 'Review of Environmental and Health Impact of Mining in Ghana,' *Journal of Health and Pollution*, Vol. 8, No. 17, March 2018, pgs. 43–52; GBN, 'Ghana, Cote d'Ivoire Work to Solve Pollution of Tano and Bia Rivers,' December 20, 2017, *Ghana Business News*, www.ghanabusinessnews.com/2017/12/20/ghana-cote-divoire-work-to-solve-pollution-of-tano-and-bia-rivers/; GAAS, 'Is Ghana on the Brink of Ecological Suicide,' *Ghana Academic of Arts and Sciences*, May 2020.
79 Tiffany Napier, 'The Effect of Sea Access on Economic Income Level in African Nations,' *Nebraska Anthropologist*, 2011, https://digitalcommons.unl.edu/cgi/viewcontent.cgi?article=1162&context=nebanthro;
80 Michael L. Faye, 'The Challenges Facing Landlocked Developing Countries,' *Journal of Human Development*, Vol. 5, No. 1, 2004, https://doi.org/10.1080/14649880310001660201
81 IOA, 'Africa's Landlocked Countries' Perpetual Disadvantage,' *In On Africa*, August 24, 2017, www.inonafrica.com/2017/08/24/africas-landlocked-countries-perpetual-disadvantage/; Antonio Ruyde Almeida Silva, 'The Enabling Power of Oceans,' *Conexto Internacional*, Vol. 39, No. 2, May/August 2017, pgs. 237–243, www.scielo.br/pdf/cint/v39n2/0102-8529-cint-2017390200002.pdf
82 Endalcachew Bayeh, 'The Legacy of Colonialism in the Contemporary Africa: A Cause for Intrastate and Interstate Conflicts,' *International Journal of Innovative and Applied Research*, Vol. 3, No. 2, 2015, pgs. 23–29.
83 Horace Campbell, *Global NATO and the Catastrophic Failure in Libya*, New York: Monthly Review, 2013.
84 Kwame Nkrumah, *Challenge of the Congo: A Case Study of Foreign Pressures in an Independent State*, New York: International Publishers, 1967.
85 Fred Grunfeld and Wessel Vermeulen, 'Failures to Prevent Genocide in Rwanda (1994), Srebrenica (1995), and Darfur (Since 2003),' Genocide Studies and Prevention: An International Journal, Vol. 4, No. 2, Article 13, August 2009, Retrieved from: https://scholarcommons.usf.edu/cgi/viewcont ent.cgi?article=1141&context=gsp.
86 Christopher M. Davidson, 'Why was Muammar Qadhafi Really Removed,' *Middle East Policy*, Vol. XXIV, No. 4, Winter 2017. Peter Koenig, 'Let's Never Forget Why Muammar Gaddafi was Killed,' Pambazuka News, May 25, 2017, Retrieved from: www.pambazuka.org/pan-africanism/let%E2%80%99s-never-forget-why-muammar-gaddafi-was-killed.
87 Makokele Nanivazo, 'Sexual Violence in the Democratic Republic of the Congo,' *United Nations University*, May 24, 2012, Retrieved from: https://unu.edu/publications/articles/sexual-violence-in-the-democratic-republic-of-the-congo.html#info.

88 Stanley Meisler, 'Prostitution Report Accuses U.N. Troops in Mozambique,' *Los Angeles Times*, February 26, 1994, Retrieved from: www.latimes.com/ archives/la-xpm-1994-02-26-mn-27378-story.html; Stewart M. Patrick and Eleanor Powell, 'Sexual Abuse by Peacekeepers: Time for Real Action,' *Council on Foreign Relations*, August 6, 2015, Retrieved from: www.cfr.org/ blog/sexual-abuse-peacekeepers-time-real-action; Sonia Elks, 'Haitians Say Under-aged Girls Were Abused by U.N. Peacekeepers,' *Reuters*, December 18, 2019.

89 Adeyinka T. Ajaji and Lateef Oluwafemi Bhuhari, 'Methods of Conflict in African Traditional Society,' *African Research Review: An International Multidisciplinary Journal, Ethiopia*,' Vol. 8, No. 2, Serial No. 33, April 2014, pgs. 138–157; Cletus A. Lanshime, 'African Traditional Systems of Conflict Resolution,' *The African Anthropologist*, Vol. 20, No.1 and 2, 2016, pgs. 262–291.

90 Paul O. Bello and Adewale A. Olutola, 'Indigenous Conflict Resolution Mechanisms in Africa: Lessons Drawn for Nigeria,' *Bangladesh e-Journal of Sociology*, Vol. 13, No. 2, July 2016, pgs. 1–19, Retrieved from: www. bangladeshsociology.org/IndigenousConflict13.2.pdf; Dejo Olowu, 'Indigenous Approaches to Conflict Resolution in Africa: A Study of the Borolong People of the North-West Province, South Africa,' *Journal of Law and Judicial System*, Vol. 1, No. 1, 2018, pgs. 10–16; Endalcachew Bayeh and Zelalen Munchie, 'Traditional Conflict Resolution Mechanisms Among Ambo Woreda Communities,' *International Journal of Research*, Vol. 1, No. 11, December 2014, pgs. 822–828.

91 Lukong Stella Shulika, 'Women and Peace Building: From Historical to Contemporary African Perspectives,' *Ubuntu: Journal of Conflict and Social Transformation*, Vol. 5, No. 1, June 2016, pgs. 7–31; Emeka Lloh et al., 'The Role of Women in Conflict Resolution in Rwanda: Lessons for Peace Building in Nigeria, April 2019, pgs. 30–41, Retrieved from: www.researchgate.net/ publication/339041476_The_Role_of_Women_in_Conflict_Resolution_in_ Rwanda_Lessons_for_Peace_Building_in_Nigeria.

92 Yilritmwa I. Goyol, 'The Role of Women in Peace-Building: Liberia in Perspective,' *International Journal of Development and Management Review*, Vol. 14, No. 1, June 2019, pgs. 123–135, Retrieved from: www.ajol.info/index. php/ijdmr/article/view/186550; Lara F. Helen Deffner, 'The Issue of Gender: Women's Roles in Sierra Leone's Civil War (1991–2002),' *Institute for Peace and Security Studies*, December 2017, retrieved from: www.researchgate. net/publication/325988700_The_Issue_of_Gender_-_Womens_Roles_in_ Sierra_Leones_Civil_War_1991-2002; Theodora-Ismene Gizelis, 'A Country of Their Own: Women and Peacebuilding,' *Journal of Conflict Resolution*, Vol. 28, No. 5, pgs. 522–542, November 2011.

93 Lansana Gberie, Review Article, ECOMOG: The Story of an Heroic Failure,' *African Affairs*, Vol. 102, No. 4, 2003, pgs. 147–154; Herbet Howe, 'Lessons of Liberia: ECOMOG and Regional Peacekeeping,' *International Security*,

Winter 1996–1997, Vol. 21, No. 3, pgs. 145–176; Michelle Pitts, 'Sub-Regional Solutions for African Conflict: The ECOMOG Experiment,' *Journal of Conflict Studies*, Vol.1, No. 1, July 1999.

94   Major Robert L. Feldman, 'Problems Plaguing the African Union Peacekeeping Forces,' *Defense and Security Analysis*, Vol. 24, No. 3, September 2008, pgs. 267–279.

95   Robin Luckman, 'French Militarism in Africa,' *Review of African Political Economy*,' May–August 1982, No. 24, pgs. 55–84; Stephen Burgess, Military Intervention in Africa: French and US Approaches Compared, ASPJ & Francophinie, 2nd Quarter, 2018, pgs. 1–21, retrieved from: www.airuniversity.af.edu/Portals/10/ASPJ_French/journals_E/Volume-09_Issue-2/burgess_e.pdf.

96   Horace Campbell, 'The United States and Security in Africa: The Impact of the Military Management of the International System,' *Africa Development*, 2017, Vol. 42, No.3, pgs. 45–71; Abel Esterhuyse, 'The Iraqization of Africa? Looking at AFRICOM from a South African Perspective,' *Strategic Studies Quarterly*, Spring 2008, pgs. 111–130.

97   Kwame Nkrumah, 'Speech at First Africanist Conference, Accra,' December 12, 1962, Reprinted in *Revolutionary Path*, New York: International, 1973, pgs. 205–217.

98   Walter Rodney, *How Europe Underdeveloped Africa*, London: Bogle-L'Ouverture, 1972.

99   Melville J. Herskovits, *The Myth of the Negro Past*, Boston: Beacon, 1941.

100 Kwame Nkrumah, *Consciencism: Philosophy and Ideology of Decolonization*, New York: Monthly Review, 1964, pgs. 70, 78–79.

101 Kwame Nkrumah, *Revolutionary Path*, op cit., pg. 205.

102 Ibid., pg. 206.

103 Oyoo Sungu, 'The AU's Dependency on Donors is a Big Shame,' Pambazuka News, June 4, 2015, retrieved from: www.pambazuka.org/governance/au%E2%80%99s-dependency-donors-big-shame; African Union, 'Sustainable Funding,' retrieved from: https://au.int/en/aureforms/financing.

104 BBC News, 'Africa Opens Chinese-Funded HQ in Ethiopia,' January 28, 2012, retrieved from: www.bbc.com/news/world-africa-16770932.

105 International Crisis Group, 'How to Spend It: New EU Funding for African Peace and Security,' Africa Report Number 297, Brussels, Belgium, January 2021, retrieved from: https://d2071andvip0wj.cloudfront.net/297-eu-au-funding-2021.pdf; Peter Fabricius, 'EU Peace and Security Funds Can Now Bypass the African Union, Institute for Security Studies,' 5 February 2021, retrieved from: https://issafrica.org/iss-today/eu-peace-and-security-funds-can-now-bypass-the-african-union.

106 African Union, *Constitutive Act of the African Union*, pgs. 7, retrieved from: https://au.int/sites/default/files/pages/34873-file-constitutiveact_en.pdf.

4 Class exploitation and socialist reconstruction in Africa

In Chapter 3, we looked at, primarily, the ginormous amount of wealth that will be created and made available for the people of Africa once a Union Government of Africa is guiding the economic affairs of the entire continent. However, this wealth, if not distributed equitably, could easily fall into the hands of an indigenous class of private land owners, entrepreneurs, corporate elites, and senior public officials whose primary purpose would be the unbridled accumulation of wealth and profit drained from exploited African labour and the pilfering of millions of dollars from state coffers. After all, the class divide in Africa today, which is hardly new, is wider than it has ever been. The roots of this divide can be traced, not over decades, but over centuries. It began in different parts of the continent with the demise of communal relations and the emergence of a class of merchants, craftsmen, traders, militarists, spiritualists, and feudal chiefs who were able to gain access to various instruments of production to advance themselves at the expense of the African majority.[1] As Nkrumah pointed out years ago

> an idyllic, African classless society (in which there were no rich and no poor) enjoying a drugged serenity is certainly a facile simplification; there is no historical or even anthropological evidence for any such society. I am afraid the realities of African society were somewhat more sordid. All available evidence from the history of Africa up to the eve of the European colonisation, shows that African society was neither classless nor devoid of a social hierarchy. Feudalism existed in some parts of Africa before colonisation; and feudalism involves a deep and exploitative social stratification, founded on the ownership of land. It must also be noted that slavery existed in Africa before European colonisation, although the earlier European contact gave slavery in Africa some of its most vicious characteristics.[2]

DOI: 10.4324/9781003224990-5

It is worth noting that the emergence of these class cleavages, which coincided with the state formation process in Africa, contributed in no small way to the deterioration in the status of women, another phenomenon that, like modern-class inequality in Africa, predates colonialism by centuries.[3]

However, it is the contemporary dimensions and character of this class divide, and the concomitant class struggle that it breeds, that we are most concerned with in this chapter (despite its organic link with earlier forms of class stratification in Africa). This modern-day class divide has become *globalized* and, unlike earlier forms of class divisions in Africa, highly *explosive*. It pits the labouring masses of African people against international finance capital, that is, imperialism, the latter of which is served by its natural allies, the African indigenous bourgeoisie, who gain, significantly, from the imperialist plunder and domination of Africa. This contemporary scenario has been the case for decades now. It began shortly after the euphoria surrounding the victory of political independence in the various microstates across Africa ended, nay, crashed. Indeed, after the cloak of national unity was lifted, nothing has been more revealing of the greed, myopia, and obedience (to their imperialist masters) of African leaders than the sham of political independence in post-colonial Africa.[4] Nkrumah's lucid summary of the nature of the class divide in Africa remains as relevant as when he first provided it:

> Class divisions in modern African society became blurred to some extent during the pre-independence period, when it seemed there was national unity and all classes joined forces to eject the colonial power. This led some to proclaim that there were no class divisions in Africa, and that the communalism and egalitarianism of traditional African society made any notion of class struggle out of the question. But the exposure of this fallacy followed quickly after independence, when class cleavages which had been temporarily submerged in the struggle to win political freedom reappeared, often with increased intensity, particularly in those states where the newly independent government embarked on socialist policies.[5]

Despite popular proclamations of neo-liberal pundits, climbing economic growth rates in several African states, accompanied by an increase in middle income earners, are not indicative, in any way, of Africa's economy breaking free of its neo-colonial chains. Nor do such indices suggest any lessening of the expanding wealth gap and class divide that are engulfing the entire continent. Indeed, this fact remains: economic *growth* is not tantamount, nor is it always the prerequisite, to economic *development*. This is especially true when economic growth is fuelled, as it is in Africa, by a reliance on mineral resource extraction and the consumption of foreign imports, both of which serve to impede African productivity. Development, on the other hand, assumes an economy that has undergone enough structural changes in its manufacturing capacity, both quantitatively and qualitatively, to be able to meet the material and immaterial needs of its people. Instead, what we have in Africa today is abundantly clear: increasing economic growth rates, accompanied by an unparalleled increase in the wealth holdings of a minority of African millionaires and billionaires, amidst spiralling poverty. This poverty is characterized by hundreds of millions of Africans being denied access to clean water, decent housing, uninterrupted power supply, quality education, affordable healthcare, and environmental safety. A recent Oxfam International study said it best:

> Despite the recent spate of economic growth, Africa remains afflicted by entrenched poverty and alarmingly high and rising inequality. The gap between rich and poor is greater than in any other region of the world apart from Latin America, and in many African countries this gap continues to grow. In this context, the prospects of achieving the Sustainable Development Goals and Agenda 2063 are severely diminished.[6]

In short, African workers, both industrial and agricultural, along with small-scale farmers, fishermen, fishmongers, public and private service workers, hawkers, market women, petty traders, and unemployed youth, the latter of who are dotting the urban landscape at an alarming rate, are being exploited by a rapacious imperialism in its neo-colonialist stage of atrophy. The systematic structures designed to maintain this exploitation have barely changed over the years—making Nkrumah's *Neo-Colonialism: The Last Stage of Imperialism* as compelling a read as ever.[7] Nor has the struggle by African labourers and their natural allies to dismantle these structures withered in the least—making Nkrumah's *Class Struggle in Africa*, where this struggle is outlined so well, as cogent an analysis as ever.[8] In this chapter, then, I would like to apply the Nkrumaist analysis by (1) summarizing some of the most current trends, patterns, and experiences—some old, some new—that characterize the nature of class exploitation in Africa today and (2) outlining the necessity for a socialist revolution that would enable the toiling masses of African people to reap the full benefits of their labour and the natural wealth of their continent.

Class exploitation in Africa

There are three major arenas where class exploitation in Africa can be understood within the context of a neo-colonized Africa: trade, aid, and investment. By reviewing these three areas, the exploitation African workers are subjected to, the complicitous role of the African bourgeoisie, and the systematic manner in which Africa, because of its division, continues to be plundered are laid bare.

Trade

With trade, after centuries of having the growth of its productive forces stunted, Africa's productive capacity, in nearly every realm, remains infantile. As a result, we continue to produce commodities for international trade which have very little or no *added value*, which, by definition, reduces their *use value* which, in turn, reduces their *exchange value* on the global market.[9] This arrangement, an economic relic of Africa's encounter with the trans-Atlantic slave trade and, afterwards, European colonialism, is at the very heart of this problem. One telling example of this, in the agricultural realm, is the failure of Mali, Burkina Faso, and Benin—three of West Africa's largest cotton growers—to advance from cotton farming to major textile manufacturing. Their failure to capture even a significant portion of the West African textile market (due largely to the lack of inter-African trade), let alone the world market, is as clear an example as any of how millions of dollars are lost when failing to add value to primary commodities. The tens of thousands of jobs that would have also been created, yet lost, is no small matter either.[10] And this is just with cotton! What about rubber, cassava, cowpeas, millet, sorghum, tomatoes, and countless other agricultural products produced in abundance, in Africa, the vast majority of which are exported in their rawest form, each one of which is also subject to the price fluctuations and demand volatility of the global market? This includes the inelasticity of demand, to which many of these commodities are also subject. More importantly, the actual prices African farmers receive for the commodities they sell, and the salaries farm labourers earn for the crops they cultivate, share no relationship to what these same commodities can (and do) earn on the international market. And herein lies the essence of class exploitation, *in trade*, under neo-colonialism in Africa!

The consortia of consuming multinational corporations of the Global North have been controlling commodity prices for decades. As a result, the prices of finished goods manufactured in the Global

North have risen consistently and significantly higher than the prices of raw unfinished goods produced in the Global South. Understood in this light, for instance, the cost of producing the amount of cotton, tomatoes, timber, and oil palm required in the production, respectively, of a pair of trousers, a can of tomato paste, a wooden cabinet, and a bar of soap is only a tiny fraction of what is earned on the international market for these processed and finished goods. Is there any wonder, then, why the chocolate industry, concentrated primarily in the Global North, where not a single cocoa tree is able to grow, generates more than $100 billion per year, while Ghana and Cote d'Ivoire, where more than 60 percent of cocoa is produced in the world, earn $2 billion and $3.7 billion, per year, respectively, roughly 5 percent of the total?[11] Their farmers (and dare we mention, here, the child labourers involved in cocoa production in both countries)[12] remain shamelessly exploited, producing a source of humongous wealth for Kit Kat, Mars, Cadbury, Toblerone, Richart, and the other top chocolate manufactures found in Switzerland, the UK, Belgium, Italy, and the United States.

Fortunately, of late, senior officials from the cocoa marketing boards of Ghana and Cote d'Ivoire have been making impressive gains in wrestling fairer prices from the powerful chocolate conglomerates, demonstrating, once again, the power of united action.[13] However, the united ad hoc efforts of just two countries hardly amount to a solution to this dilemma, which is continental in scope. Nkrumah learned this lesson years ago in this same cocoa industry:

> As experience with the Cocoa Producers Alliance has shown, any organization which is based on a mere commercial agreement between primary producers is insufficient to secure a fair world price. This can only be obtained when the united power of the producer countries is harnessed by common political and economic policies and has behind it the united financial resources of the States concerned.
>
> So long as Africa remains divided it will therefore be the wealthy consumer countries who will dictate the price of African cash crops.[14]

And, in fact, these same officials in Ghana and Cote d'Ivoire are just recently learning much of the same: Hershey Company, one of the largest chocolate manufacturers in the world, decided to buy cocoa on the futures market to avoid paying the mutually agreed increase in cocoa prices.[15]

The class exploitation in Africa's vast mineral sector, driven by the global trade in these commodities, is not significantly different from the exploitation carried out in its agricultural sector. However, the level of sexual violence, state repression, and militarism associated with, and used to maintain, the higher levels of exploitation in the mineral sector does warrant special attention. The regional battle for gold, columbite-tantalite, and other critical mineral resources in the Eastern Region of the Democratic Republic of the Congo—spearheaded by elite politicians and money-hungry warlords—is perhaps the most recent and tragic example.[16] Mass rapes, kidnaping, looting, child labour, and the rampant destruction of homes and personal property of innocent civilians have been the horrendous plight of those with the misfortune of being from that part of mineral-rich Congo! And like their counterparts in the agricultural sector, African miners receive barely a pittance of what these minerals earn when traded on the global market. Indeed, thanks to the extreme exploitation of African miners, the cost of extracting the amount of bauxite, manganese, coltan, and cobalt required in the production, respectively, of a slate of aluminium, a steel rod, a cell phone, and a jet engine is only a tiny fraction of what is earned on the international market for these finished goods.

The platinum trade in South Africa provides, still, another glaring example. The 34 striking miners shot at the Marikana platinum mine by South African police—mostly in their back, while running—would have certainly concurred had they survived.[17] So too would one of the lucky survivors of this brutal massacre who gave voice to why this wildcat strike was taking place: 'We are exploited, [and] neither the government nor the unions have come to help us ... The mining companies make money thanks to our work and they pay us practically nothing. We are not offered a decent life. We live like animals because of our poverty wages.'[18] Indeed, African platinum miners saw very little of the huge profits made by the privately owned platinum mines in South Africa during the commodity boom of the first decade of the new millennium.[19] And even when the boom ended, these companies (and their shareholders) have continued to make handsome profits while sharing very little with those who continue to sweat it out in hot, stuffy, and dangerous holes in the ground.[20] Variations of this same experience are shared by labourers in the diamond mines in Sierra Leone, uranium mines in Niger, gold mines in Ghana, copper mines in Zambia, phosphate mines in the Western Sahara, and bauxite mines in Guinea and Mozambique, to name but a few.

Aid

Prolonged balance of payments deficits is the systemic outcome for African states caught in the quagmire of international trade. The export earnings that fill their public coffers, derived from the commodities they sell to the predatory nations of the Global North, will never be enough to pay for the constantly increasing prices of imported manufactured goods, nor be enough to contribute, significantly, to the costs of meeting the quality of life needs of their people. As discussed earlier, this stark reality is built into the system of international trade. After all, as Akinwumi Adesina, president of the African Development Bank, has witnessed:

> The price of cotton may decline, but never the price of textile and garments. The price of cocoa may decline but never the price of chocolates. The price of coffee beans may decline but never the price of brewed specialty coffee at Starbucks.[21]

Hence, for all of the reasons discussed earlier, a divided Africa remains in debt and unable to pay for the goods and services required to meet the expanding needs of its exponentially growing population. These needs are especially acute in Africa's sprawling urban centres, where huge and expensive infrastructural projects have begun in an effort to address major problems in healthcare, education, waste management, road construction, and power supply, among others. And thus we have arrived at the *raison d'etre* for Africa's incessant need for external support, that is, foreign aid and its fraternal, nay, evil twin, relentless borrowing! As in the case with international trade, these two conjoin in various ways to exploit African labour and expropriate Africa's wealth.

In fact, foreign aid to Africa has been disastrous, especially those aid packages—read: tools of neo-colonialism—that have been crafted by the nations and institutions of the Global North.[22] However, even the more benevolent packages that have been provided—more recently by China[23]—have only served to reinforce the same problem that foreign aid causes in Africa: dependency! This dependency, discussed further below, is both financial and psychological. Then, too, how (disgraceful) does it look for the leaders of so-called sovereign nations—nations endowed with more natural wealth and industrial potential than the nations to whom they are appealing for aid—to be always begging, year in and year out, hat in hand, on bended knee, for financial handouts from other sovereign nations (and the financial institutions these nations control)? What message does this send, subliminally, to African youth, in whose hands Africa's future belongs? Africa as a continent inhabited by helpless, complacent, unimaginative, and uncivilized people immediately has to come to mind. On top of this, the sad truth of the matter is that there is an abundance of data indicating that this aid has done far more harm in Africa, economically, than good, serving merely to enhance Africa's underdevelopment.[24] This tragedy has been eloquently summarized, below, by Itai Kabonga:

> donor aid is the embodiment of the dependency that exists between the richer and poorer countries. The unabated flow of resources from the periphery to the core countries has enriched the core, dialectically impoverishing the periphery. In the same manner, the flow of donor aid from richer countries to the poorer countries paradoxically has enriched the richer countries, further condemning poorer countries to scathing poverty. Aid has created a situation where Third World countries have become dependent on donors as solution bearers to multifarious problems compounding them. Aid has become a tool for the development of underdevelopment; for it is creating more employment and demand for services and goods in the core countries than in the periphery.[25]

In short, the damages this aid has caused Africa, especially to its public at-large, and to its working people in particular, are as voluminous as they are multifarious. Below, in three broad areas, is an attempt to summarize these damages as succinctly as possible.

First and foremost are the conditionalities upon which this aid is given.[26] After the first two decades of independence, after ignoring Nkrumah's dire warning to 'unify or perish,'[27] a weak, divided, and financially insolvent Africa came under the ideological control of neoliberalism: the Global North's financial prescription of how to 'fix' Africa's economic woes. Indeed, since the 1980s, the conditionalities the IMF, the World Bank, and other single and multilateral donors have imposed, and continue to impose, on Africa in one form or another, under one guise or another, have been horrendous. Under the guiding rubric of free market capitalism, these five major (interwoven) pillars, encapsulated below, serve as the foundation of these debilitating conditionalities.

1 **Privatization**[28]
    African Governments have had to sell off their state run enterprises, including those that were profitable, resulting in a significant loss of state revenue and public sector jobs in companies that were

downsized. Moreover, these enterprises were sold primarily to foreign investors—all of whom were allowed to repatriate their profits abroad without being required to reinvest in local African economies. Even some state run utilities were privatized, for example, public water supply companies, which, because of the higher prices charged, resulted in decreased access to water among the poor which, in turn, led to an increase in water-borne diseases, for example, cholera, as people began using unsafe and unhealthy water supplies. The privatization of electricity has been equally as damaging for those countries that privatized their power companies: increased energy prices have led to greater use of charcoal which, in turn, has increased deforestation.

2 **Trade liberalization**[29]

African infant and small-scale industries, unlike their counterparts in space and time, have not been provided the protection from the competition of the industrial giants of the Global North (and elsewhere), whose benefits from government subsidies and economies of scale (because of the large markets they serve) are not available to African producers. In short, goods produced in the factories and plants of the Global North—from toothpicks to tractors, from processed rice to frozen chicken—have been able to enter the African market, unencumbered, without the financial burden of duties and tariffs.

3 **Control of monetary policy**[30]

For the past 40 years, the value of African currencies has been under the (compulsory) tutelage of the aid donors and money lenders of the Global North. And regardless of the instructions given—from devaluation to free floating—African currencies, because of the poor performance of Africa's manufacturing sector, have consistently fallen against all major currencies. The impact this has had on the salaries of African labourers has been disastrous, especially with the (double-digit) inflationary pressure this puts on economies so heavily dependent on imports (as is Africa's plight).

4 **Reduced government regulations and spending**[31]

To ensure that monies borrowed will be paid back to their neo-colonial lenders (at exorbitant interest rates), African governments have been required to reduce public spending on education, healthcare, salaries and hiring, and the delivery of basic public services. This has resulted in teachers, nurses, and doctors not getting paid or not receiving badly needed pay increases. Farm subsidies, too, have been largely wiped out, making it very difficult for African farmers to compete with their (subsidized) counterparts in the Global

North. And in various African states, government regulations that were designed to protect the rights of workers have been steadily removed.

5   **Tied aid**[32]

An overwhelming amount of foreign aid to Africa never leaves the donor nations. Instead, African states receiving this 'aid' are required to purchase goods and services from the donor nation which, ironically, provides income and jobs for citizens of the donor nation and huge profits for the firms providing these goods and services. Moreover, in many cases the goods and services being purchased are not only not appropriate to the project being funded in the recipient country; they are often significantly more expensive than what is available in the recipient country, arrive late, and cause harmful delays.

The second major damage this aid has caused Africa is the manner in which Africa has become so utterly dependent upon it.[33] And like any addict who believes he cannot function without receiving the very substance of what abuses him, and what he is addicted to, African heads of states and their ministerial advisors have mastered the habit of laying the continent prostrate at the door of the foreign aid cartel. It is in their class interests to provide this type of leadership given the huge financial gains they have accrued in managing Africa's economy in this way. However, it is the *degree* of vulnerability this class of recreants has rendered the continent that has made Africa's dependency on foreign aid so much worst. After the failure of countless World Bank grants to solve Africa's development challenges, the level of dependency on further grants, and the endless supplication for IMF loans (and other credit facilities, including the now popular Eurobonds), has been described by even some reformist economists as absurd:

> Helping Africa is a noble cause, but the campaign has become a theater of the absurd—the blind leading the clueless. The record of Western aid to Africa is one of abysmal failure. More than $500 billion in foreign aid—the equivalent of four Marshall Aid Plans—was pumped into Africa between 1960 and 1997. Instead of increasing development, aid has created dependence. The budgets of Ghana and Uganda, for example, are more than 50 percent aid dependent.[34]

In addition to lowering the per capita GDP of the recipient states, the foreign debt to GDP ratio in these same states has exceeded the threshold for any rational opportunity for development. How can Ghana, for example, the supposed darling of African development success, develop with a debt-GDP ratio of 76.7 percent, owing more than $24 billion dollars to various foreign creditors?[35] The interest payments for this debt in 2020, alone, was over $5.2 billion! Where, then, will the resources come from to finance what's urgently needed in Ghana in the areas of education, healthcare, agriculture, sanitation, road construction, power supply, and various other areas of human need. It certainly will not come from her volatile export earnings which, as outlined earlier, have never been enough. And Ghana, by far, is not alone in this dilemma, especially in light of the devastating impact COVID-19 is having on the entire continent.[36] What better wake-up call is there for Africa to unite and pool its resources than a global pandemic that is exposing, more than ever, its bankruptcy and destitution?

Corruption, the third major area of damage foreign aid is causing Africa, is no less serious than the previous two discussed. In fact, it is in this area where the pillaging of the African ruling elite, in both the private and public sectors, may be the most apparent. Needless to say, corruption is a global phenomenon, practiced more in the Global North, perhaps, than anywhere else.[37] However, the circumstances in Africa are different, rendering its ruling elite more inclined to kleptocracy than their counterparts in the Global North. The wide variety of options of exploiting labour, which characterize capital–labour relations in the Global North (with their innumerous factories and plants), are not as available to the African ruling class, given the diminutive size of the African manufacturing sector. Consequently, the African *political* elite, especially, find it expedient to take advantage of their access to the billions of dollars in foreign aid and loans that pour into Africa every year.

Moreover, there are a number of institutional weaknesses in most African states that provide numerous opportunities for the African elite to fleece billions of dollars from foreign aid, loan monies, and the general government revenue.[38] They include, minimally, the following three: (1) the executive, judicial, and legislative systems consistently fail to indict, convict, and sentence the African elite who commit white-collar crimes, such as fraud, bribery, embezzlement, and money laundering; (2) political patronage has taken deep roots throughout the continent, especially among public sector institutions, including both the executive and legislative branches of government; (3) the paucity and impotency of civic institutions make it very difficult for the public at-large to hold senior public officials accountable for financial malfeasance.[39]

With an estimated annual loss, in Africa, of $148 billion to corruption,[40] the blatant pillaging of the ruling elite from state treasuries in Africa is tantamount to the exploitation of labour that occurs routinely in the Global North and anywhere else in the world. For at the end of the day, this stolen wealth, provided in the form of foreign aid and loans to African governments, is ultimately derived from the exploited labour of those who toil in the fields and in the mines across Africa.

Investment

The exploitation of labour under the guise of foreign direct investment (FDI) has been taking place in *independent* Africa for nearly a century. It began in 1926 when Harvey S. Firestone acquired 1 million acres of land, on lease, from the Liberian government for 99 years at 6 cents per acre! Despite the multi-billions of dollars in revenue the Firestone Tire and Rubber Company has earned from the exploitation of Liberian labourers over the years, children (once again) included, there is absolutely nothing in Liberia to show for it unless we consider the damage that has been done to the Farmington River and surrounding towns and villages, adjacent to the Firestone Rubber plantation.[41] The chemical waste that has been released into the waterbodies of these communities has made life dreadful for residents who depend on these waterways for fishing, bathing, and drinking water. The human and environment exposure to the compounds and chemicals involved in latex processing has also been linked to cancer, birth defects, infertility, respiratory damage, and other serious diseases in those communities.

In fact, in many ways, the experience of Firestone in Liberia serves as the original template for how FDI has performed in post-colonial Africa. This template includes four basic components, summarized below, all of which were perfected, first, by Firestone, and practiced later by a legion of corporate successors who, on Trojan Horses, have been cruising into various African states since independence:

1   **Investment friendly environment**[42]
    In order to court FDI, African states, under the bloated assumption that FDI will bring significant benefits to their economies, are compelled to provide as many financial incentives as possible to attract these subsidiaries of multinational corporations to invest in their countries. Some of these enticements include tax holidays, repatriation of profits (without being required to invest in the local

economy), low interest or interest-free bank loans, low-leasing land acquisitions, and government deregulation. Firestone Rubber and Tire Company in Liberia, a subsidiary of Bridgestone Americas, Inc., has benefitted from all of the above. The manner in which these incentives have intensified the exploitation and oppression of African Labourers, by depriving them of the wealth they've created and alienating them from their land, is incalculable.

2 **Mineral and raw materials extraction**[43]

Unlike in other parts of the world, especially in Asia, FDI in Africa has centred overwhelmingly around the extraction of mineral resources and raw materials, especially around oil and natural gas. And as established by Firestone in Liberia, where not a single tire-producing factory has been built, value-adding has not been a requirement for foreign direct investors in Africa. This largely explains why so little technology transference occurs when foreign companies invest in Africa (as compared to China). In this way, production remains labour-intense and dirt cheap.

3 **Environmental damage**[44]

The FDI record of damages to Africa's ecosystem and the health of its population is infamous. Oil companies in Nigeria, for example, average one oil spill per week, far above the global average. The unprotected exposure to raw, radioactive uranium of miners in Niger, causing sickness and death from uranium-related cancers, is equally as tragic. These, and others, are due, in no small measure, to the investment-friendly enticement of weak regulatory policies. Deforestation from lumber companies, river contamination from mining investors, forced migration from hydroelectric projects, and air pollution from toxic emissions released from processing plants also represent a significant part of the problem. Sadly, many of these operations are illicit and, thus, go unnoticed by the public at-large. Then, when combined with the disproportionate impact climate change is having on Africa, especially on its common labourers, the environmental threats of FDI in Africa loom wider.

4 **Labour exploitation**[45]

With the complicitous role of the African ruling class as facilitators *par excellence*, the primary purpose of FDI in post-colonial Africa, the exploitation of African workers, has been realized *ad infinitum*. The countless number of raw materials and mineral resources, so abundantly available in continental Africa, require, at minimum, labour power for growing, cultivating, harvesting and, with minerals, extraction. And for this sweat and toil, African labourers, like labourers around the world, have served as a gigantesque source of wealth multiple times more than what they have received in wages.

To be clear, there is absolutely nothing inherently wrong in trading with other countries; providing aid for, and receiving aid from, other countries; and allowing other countries to invest in your own country. However, in all cases, *size* matters, *power* matters, and *leadership* matters. China, of course, provides the best example of this, where FDI has to adhere to several regulatory policies, one of which includes technology sharing. Moreover, to gain access to the Chinese market of 1.4 billion people, foreign companies are often required to build their products *in China*, and often with joint partnerships with the Chinese government or with local private entrepreneurs.[46] And because of China's market size, industrial power, and patriotic leadership, companies in the Global North (and elsewhere) have largely complied. After all, what multinational corporation would not covet access to such a huge market of rapidly growing middle-income earners, even if it meant some degree of technology sharing? Fiat Chrysler Automobiles (FCA) certainly did not mind meeting these requirements. It has been selling, annually, over 150,000 of its cars, *built in China*, to the Chinese people in the largest auto sector in the world, earning more than $100 billion per annum.[47] And along the way, FCA has been compelled to transfer the technology required in making electric cars to Chinese hands—a veritable win-win scenario.

As discussed at length in Chapter 3, Africa will be able to do much the same, and more, once a Union Government of Africa is established.

Socialist reconstruction in Africa

Uniting Africa for the purpose of enhancing the accumulation of wealth for Africa's *nouveau riche* (in both the private and public sectors) will never do. In fact, if, under the auspices of a Union Government of Africa, this grave potential is not arrested, the bourgeoning class divide that is causing so much misery and suffering for the African majority will only escalate. Considering the history of capitalist exploitation *vis a vis* Africa and its people, the remedy is clear: socialist reconstruction. This is why Nkrumah never conceived of achieving African unity under a capitalist economic system. On the contrary, for him, 'At the core of the concept of African unity lies socialism and the socialist definition of the new African society.'[48] According to Nkrumah, 'Socialism and African unity are organically complementary.'[49] Indeed, it is difficult to imagine how anyone who is relatively conscious would need much convincing to understand just how inimical the capitalist system has been to the development of Africa and its scattered and suffering people. Besides it being inherently exploitative, there is the link between the European slave trade and capitalism, the former having provided the lion's share of the wealth, that is, original accumulation of capital, that helped to finance the industrial revolution and gave birth to the capitalist system between the sixteenth and seventeenth centuries;[50] and then there is the expansion of the capitalist system, itself, into imperialism, culminating, formally, for Africa at least, at the Belin Conference in 1884–1885.[51]

In short, providing a capitalist incubator for the breeding of a class of rich tycoons, in both the public and private sectors, is in complete contradiction to the aims and objectives of the Pan-African movement. The incessant pursuit of wealth and profit from this class of indigenous plunderers would supersede the importance of everything else in life, including life itself, causing pain, suffering, and destruction across the continent. Conversely, socialist reconstruction in Africa will, perforce, include policies designed to (1) reclaim the stolen wealth being drained from the mines, fields, plantations, and factories across Africa from multinational corporations and their indigenous partners; and (2) reverse the land-grabbing operations across Africa, facilitated by the ruling elite, that have caused the loss of nearly 100 million hectares of land throughout Africa to various countries and corporations from abroad.[52] Without the implementation of these measures, there would be no other way to finance universal healthcare, universal education, universal housing, and various other programmes designed to meet the material and immaterial needs of the African people—not least of which would include reversing the environmental degradation of the continent.

Socialism, like capitalism, its opposite, is an economic system with universally abiding principals. Its primary objective is to ensure that the natural resources and wealth of a nation are used, exclusively, for the material and immaterial benefits of all its people. In that labour is the source of all wealth of any nation, including both physical and mental labour, socialism is not an economic system designed to meet the pecuniary interests of a minority of a nation's population, *enabling* them, through private ownership of the means of production, to become multiples of millionaires and billionaires. Instead, socialism is designed to meet the holistic needs of the entirety of a nation's population.[53] The primary method of ensuring that majority needs are met is by *denying* private ownership of the means of production to a small minority of the population, and placing it, instead, in the hands of the people. In this way—with factories, plants, machines, equipment, mineral resources, and the complete body of instruments of production placed under the ownership and in the command of the public good—poverty and want, hunger and ignorance, can be eliminated.

However, despite its universality, the particular road or path to socialism, under a Union Government of Africa, will have to be determined by the particular circumstances facing Africa in the first quarter of the twenty-first century. This, in fact, is what socialist nations have been charged with since their existence: 'To devise policies aimed at general socialist goals, which take their form from the concrete, specific circumstances and conditions of a particular country at a definite historical period.'[54] For Africa, these circumstances would embody, broadly, a mixture of factors, including, at minimum, Africa's unique topography and geography, which have contributed significantly to its cultural patterns; its historical legacy, which has resulted from Africa's battles with internal and external forces and from its relationship with two of the major religions of the world, viz., Islam and Christianity; and its position in the contemporary world, which is a reflection of the adverse effects globalization, and the dire impact of climate change, are having on the continent.

In light of the conditions and circumstances described earlier, a brief outline of five broad areas socialist reconstruction policies will have to address under an African Union Government is discussed below.

Transitional period

Without exception, nations that have been in the throes of building a socialist economy have done so incrementally, in stages. Moreover, these nations have undergone this process under extreme duress, harrowing their way in the midst of an inhospitable global climate of capitalist hegemony. This is partly why so few have succeeded, some have failed, and others have found the realization of socialist goals elusive at best. Furthermore, from the collapse of the erstwhile Soviet Union to the contemporary plight of Venezuela and Cuba, socialist economies have inherited an economic condition neither Marx nor Engels had envisioned: technological and industrial underdevelopment. Indeed, the two leading nineteenth-century socialist theoreticians had reasoned that socialist revolution would take place, first, in advanced capitalist countries.[55] According to Marx and Engels, under late capitalism the *productive forces*, that is, the skills, technology, tools, machines, science, equipment, and so on, which are dynamic and never to be stymied, would be so advanced that they would come into conflict with the more stagnant capitalist *relations of production*, that is, the arrangement that allows for a minute percentage of the population to privately own the means of production. The big conflict, or irreconcilable contradiction, would derive from the owners in this market economy being unable to utilize the productive forces in ways that would be profitable for them. In short, socialist revolution would occur, according to the two pundits, when the market-driven capitalist economy of private ownership, plagued with the internal contradiction of eroding its own market demand, would no longer be able to engage the productive forces in ways that would nurture their further development and create profitable investments for the owners. As a result, shops, factories, and plants would shut down, and the angry, hungry workers would eventually get organized and make revolution. However, this particular scenario, as reasonable as it may sound, never served as the precondition for those revolutionary leaders of nations that, under incredible stress and turmoil, were able to usher in a socialist path of development.

These conditions are not found in Africa either. How, then, do we develop Africa's productive forces under a socialist reconstruction model without benefiting, at least early on, at least partially, from the technology-boosting effects of private ownership of the means of production, the hallmark of the capitalist system? And how, too, do we avoid suffering from the debilitating impact this same system has on human life. After all, the neo-colonial economy a socialist Africa will be inheriting is severely lacking in its productive capacity to provide the wide variety of goods and services required to meet the basic needs of its 1.3 billion people. This dilemma, in one form or another, has befuddled them all, beginning in the Soviet Union with V.I Lenin, who, in 1921, four years after the Great October Revolution, was forced to introduce the New Economic Policy (NEP).[56] NEP restored significant portions of the market economy, while allowing for private ownership, via leasing and state trusts, of certain portions of Russia's inchoative industry. And while China's 40-year experiment of 'Socialism with Chinese Characteristics' has lifted more than 800 million Chinese out of poverty, how high a price has she paid?[57] Much the same could be speculated about the Vietnamese transitional policy of *Doi Moi*, that is, 'Socialist Market Economy under State Guidance.'[58] In both cases, as a direct result of the state controlled market economies that were introduced, the improvement in the quality of life of millions of their citizens has been amazing, especially regarding the major human development indices of life expectancy, literacy rates, and per capita income. However, as in the case with China, a widening income gap, the resurgence of class cleavages, and the toxic impact a market-driven economy has on the environment have become very real threats to the Vietnamese socialist revolution.

The external and internal challenges facing a Union Government of Africa in its transitional phase to socialism will be much the same, if not greater. Externally, there is no reason to even imagine that the global environment will be any less congenial to Africa's effort in removing itself from the clutches of imperialist domination than it has been to other nations who have forged similar efforts. Consulting with comrades in Cuba and Venezuela, today, and learning from the historical experiences of others from the past, would provide helpful insights. Indeed, their experiences with fighting against the relentless efforts of the imperialist nations to reverse the gains of their socialist revolutions—including, among various schemes, providing tacit and blatant support for internal opposition—are well known and worthy of paramount attention. Clearly, the political leadership of the Union Government of Africa will have its hands full!

Internally, Africa's productive forces, which are far too inadequate to provide the vast amount, and wide variety, of goods and services needed by Africa's teeming millions, will need to be revved up as quickly as possible. The quality of life indices in Africa that socialist reconstruction policies will have to address, immediately, reveal just how critical the challenges will be during this transitional period. Indeed, sadly, Africa is at the bottom quintile, globally, of all the human development indices that genuinely matter: life expectancy, access to clean and safe water, living in poverty, access to formal healthcare, per capita income, access to electricity, living under sanitary conditions, infant mortality rate, and percentage of children attending primary school.[59] In this regard, it would be worth revisiting Ghana's 7-Year Development Plan, aka, 'Programme for Work and Happiness,' first launched in 1962. It remains one of the best African-centred socialist transition programmes designed to enhance Africa's productive capacity.[60] Its five-sectored economy, which included state *and* private enterprises, was based on the premise, stated earlier, that '… there are many roads to socialism, and in the circumstances of our present retardedness, we must employ all the forces at our disposal while we fashion others which will accelerate our progress towards our goal.'[61] Had these plans not been derailed by Nkrumah's removal in 1966, thanks to the CIA (financed and orchestrated) coup d'état,[62] Ghana's transition to socialism, in time, despite errors made, despite Ghana's small size, would have made significant progress in developing the country's productive forces.

Gender Oppression

'The degree of a country's revolutionary awareness may be measured by the political maturity of its women,' wrote Kwame Nkrumah in 1968.[63] Lenin sounded the same alarm when he spoke at the First All-Russia Congress of Working Women exactly 50 years earlier: 'The experience of all liberation movements has shown that the success of a revolution depends on how much the women take part in it.'[64] Sékou Touré, Nkrumah's Pan-African compatriot in Guinea, was equally as clear in his writings on the liberation of African women: 'A man is never emancipated so long as his female companion is not.'[65] Amy Ashwood Garvey put it equally as succinct and powerful: 'A nation without great women is a nation frolicking in peril.'[66] However, it is probably Mao Zedong's famous proclamation that captures this axiom best: 'Women hold up half the sky!' Needless to say, legions of women, with their voices and in their actions, have testified to this truth ever since Homo sapiens began populating planet earth. With over half of Africa's population being female, the implications of the maxims above must be at the top of the list of challenges to be addressed by socialist reconstruction policies and programmes in post-neo-colonial Africa.

What must be done by the Union Government of Africa in this regard is both simple and complex. It is simple in that what will be required of the government is to ensure, through legislation and enforcement, that equal rights and equal opportunities for all women, in all spheres of life, are guaranteed and protected, and that women are never subjected to the institutionalized violence so prevalent in male-dominated Africa. What will be more complicated and difficult to achieve, however, is to reverse and eliminate the deeply imbedded cultural values and patterns of behaviour, in both men and women, that have served to buttress the oppression of women since the breakdown of communal societies across Africa. In short, the marginalization, inhibition, and subordination of women did not begin in the modern era of globalization and neo-liberalism. On the contrary, the pre-colonial, colonial, and neo-colonial periods have all played their parts in the subjugation of the women of Africa—all of which have the common thread of separating women from the socio-economic resources in society that are required to make a living, for example, land, tools, skills, technology, credit, and income.[67] Moreover, the patriarchy so prevalent in Islam, Christianity, Western European culture, and, to some extent, traditional African culture have all served to reinforce and legitimize, ideologically, this separation.[68]

Hence, the complexity of the task for the Union Government in struggling to build a socialist Africa! Regardless, there are at least three major (closely related) areas, in no particular order, that will require immediate attention:[69]

1 **Empowerment**
   Through primarily their own efforts, the women of Africa must be empowered to impact the social order in ways that will ensure their equal treatment and equal access to all opportunities that will enable them to reach their fullest potential. Government must assist, especially by supporting the countless number of grassroots organizations, led by women activists, that are already contributing to the empowerment of women. Women will also have to hold government positions in proportion to their representation in the population, including all branches of government, including local, regional, and federal levels. This will ensure that legislation is passed *and* enforced to rid African society of child marriages, FGM, ritual servitude, domestic violence, iniquitous inheritance practices, and any other traditional, foreign, or capitalist practices that serve to subjugate and disempower females. This would include gender-based salary structures, and any other legal or traditional hindrances that would impede women from working in fields that have been historically denied them. In short, the economic and political dependency women have on men must be completely broken!

2 **Healthcare**
   Women in Africa, who work anywhere between 15 and 18 hours per day (weeding, farming, collecting water and firewood, processing, storing, and transporting food, while also assuming several domestic responsibilities), whose health needs are the least likely to be served in Africa, and who have some of the highest infant and maternal death rates in the world, must be provided free and high-quality healthcare services. These services must include excellent reproductive care, including contraceptive care and free and safe abortions upon their request. This is the socialist standard!

3 **Education**
   Free and compulsory education for males and females from the ages of 6 to 16, from primary to secondary levels, must be provided and mandated throughout the continent. Women must be encouraged to join the ranks of their male counterparts at the tertiary level as well, all of which must be made free by the Union Government of Africa. Moreover, in order to enhance our agricultural yields, educational training in Africa, for women, must include the provision of technological skills that have, historically, been denied to African female farmers. Furthermore, mass public, well-funded educational

campaigns must be organized to educate the entire African population—of youth and adults, male and female—to eradicate those backward attitudes and beliefs about the innate inferiority of females and natural superiority of males. The mediums available to promote this message are extensive, and must be used to replace the senseless and wasteful advertisements of frivolous products and services that bombard the public consciousness under market-driven capitalism.

As difficult as it may be, dismantling gender oppression in Africa must include banning discrimination based on sexual orientation and gender identity as well. Sexual relations between same-sex consenting adults is no one's business besides those consenting adults. In short, every effort must be made to uproot homophobia and transphobia that are currently widespread in Africa. The new united socialist Africa will not only need the entirety of its population working, unencumbered, for the development of the continent; it cannot, on the basis of egalitarianism and humanism, deny any citizen, nay, human being, the dignity of being accorded complete, unadulterated civil and human rights.

Distribution of wealth

In the case of Africa, the creation of wealth is not a problem at all. As Nkrumah was fond of saying, 'It is not that Africa is poor. It is Africans, who are impoverished by centuries of exploitation and domination,' who are poor.[70] Hence, one of the first duties the Union Government of Africa will have to perform is the nationalization of those financial institutions where the majority of this wealth is created. As Nkrumah has put it, succinctly, 'The idea is not to destroy or dismantle the network of foreign mining complexes and industrial companies throughout Africa, but to take them over and operate them in the sole interest of the African peoples.'[71] The extent and speed by which this wealth is *captured*, and the modalities used to ensure its distribution to the African majority, will require extensive continent-wide planning. And, as indicated earlier, this process will inevitably be shaped by the history, culture, and extant conditions facing Africa and its people at the time power is seized.

Fortunately, the arsenal of institutional instruments available in Africa to ensure that this wealth is generated *and* distributed equitably is fully loaded. Profits from the wide array of state-owned enterprises coupled with taxes on profits from private-operated enterprises, alone, will serve the Union Government well in *capturing* much of Africa's wealth. Indeed, even conservative accounts estimate that Africa, today, could earn at least $110 billion, annually, from just tax revenues.[72] Billions more will be added when collection capacity is increased, corruption is addressed, enforcement is strengthened, and the millions of workers in the informal sector are moved to the formal sector. The trillions of dollars to be earned, annually, from the profits on Africa's mineral wealth and agricultural potential, discussed at length in Chapter 3, will also be at the fingertips of the African majority. On the distribution side of the coin, this wealth will have to include, minimally, the provision of universal healthcare; free public education; subsidized housing; pensions and various retirement benefits for the elderly; fixed (reduced) pricing on food; access to uninterrupted power supply; and the constant availability of public services to ensure that everyone is drinking safe water, living in a clean sanitary environment, and free of the political and economic insecurities that plague the lives of countless millions.

Environmental protection

Of all the challenges that will have to be addressed with Africa's recaptured wealth, the ecological damage being done to our planet, and the catastrophic impact this damage is having on Africa, may be the greatest. Without a gigantic effort of environmental recovery, the continuous and calamitous destruction of Africa's biodiversity will serve to undermine the realization of Pan-African aims and objectives. For this reason, with haste, diligence, and an abundance of financial resources, the degradation of soils, destruction of forests, contamination of water bodies, and pollution of air quality in Africa—coupled with and caused (partially) by global warming—will have to be arrested forthwith. Placing the nation's primary interest in the quality of life of its people over pursuing the insatiable demand for commercial profits, one of the cornerstones of the socialist system, should help.[73] Otherwise, nature will have its requital, and bestow to its violators food insecurity, forced migrations, health crises, and the loss of entire livelihoods. In short, maintaining the environmental integrity of continental Africa has to be an integral part of the Pan-African imperative!

Two sectors of the African population will be most important in this endeavour. First, involving the youth in this gigantic effort makes perfect sense. Indeed, this cause must not only become an integral part of their school curricular, from primary to tertiary levels; it must also include various practical exercises designed to empower them in the defence of the continent's environmental future. These activities can include youth conducting scientific research, clean-up exercises, recycling competitions, tree planting operations, mass rallies, and educational seminars, to name but few. Second, the critical role of women in the protection of the environment must also not be overlooked![74] In fact, their ability to impact climate change, in general, and to reduce carbon emissions, in particular, is tremendous, especially in how they cook, farm, collect and store water, and eliminate waste. In these daily household activities, carried out almost exclusively by women, the Union Government of Socialist Africa—with training, and under the guidance, of women—can reboot how common ordinary folk relate to the African environment. These basic, grassroots activities should serve as the basis upon which all efforts in protecting the African environment must be forged.

Governance

The ultimate goal of Pan-Africanism, a united and socialist Africa, will need a system of governance in place to ensure its sustenance and the full realization of its objectives. The enemies of Pan-Africanism, from within the continent and without, will not lie idle as labour begins to dominate capital, as the various tentacles of neo-colonialism are dismembered and permanently discarded, and as Africa's wealth is recaptured and redistributed to the African majority. The 'Withering away of the State,' one of the theoretical pillars of orthodox socialism,[75] may very well happen, but certainly not in the foreseeable future. Imperialism, especially in its final neo-colonialist stage, has proven to be far more tenacious than most socialist theoreticians imagined and many activists considered. Consequently, a strong, unitary, democratic state, 'capable of exercising a central authority for the mobilization of the national effort and the co-ordination of reconstruction and progress,'[76] will be an absolute necessity. The African bourgeoisie, with the full economic, political, and military support of its global allies, will need to be neutralized by the new Union Government of Africa before the neo-colonialist system is completely dismantled. The mischief this class is capable of creating, for years to come, should not be taken lightly.

However, what must be rejected in pursuit of the Pan-African agenda, at all costs, is the use of the multiparty system of government inherited from the former colonial rulers. This form of government has caused tremendous harm in post-colonial Africa. Based on the premise of 'winner takes all,' multi-partyism, especially in Africa, encourages sycophancy, patronage, and nepotism while impeding the ability of persons to hold office with demonstrable abilities, expertise, and merit. Indeed, ministerial positions in Africa, along with other critically important governmental posts, are routinely held, exclusively, by party stalwarts who, more often than not, have little or no knowledge, experience, or proficiency in the affairs to which they have been assigned. Furthermore, this system, being so expensive and wasteful to operate, requires candidates running for parliament and the presidency to pay exorbitant amounts of money to their respective parties, to national electoral commissions, and to advertising agencies to promote their candidacy.[77] This, in turn, rules out persons with meagre funds to hold office, despite their qualifications. As outlined below, this system has also proven to be extremely disruptive, destructive, divisive, and destabilizing.

1   Disruptive
The major problems and challenges facing Africa are generational, and will take several years, if not decades, of uninterrupted commitment, financial and otherwise, to solve. These problems certainly cannot be 'fixed' within the 4–5 years politicians in the multiparty system of government have before their term ends and the next election cycle begins (despite their promises of doing so). In fact, shortly after the middle of their term, they have to begin planning for their next election bid. This requires that policies and programmes with short-term life spans be designed to ensure victory during the next election cycle, regardless of whether or not these policies and programmes provide long-term and widespread benefit to the nation. On other occasions, programmes started by one party that require several years or more to reach their fullest potential, will either be curtailed or abandoned by a rival party during a subsequent term in office, regardless of the programmes' worthiness. This disruptive cycle continues every 4–5 years, *ad infintum*, throughout the continent.

2   Destructive
There is hardly an election held in Africa under the banner of Western-styled multi-partyism that is not marred by violence, which often includes the destruction of people's lives and property. The usual pattern revolves around the party in power utilizing the state's use of force to harass, bully, arrest, or kill the followers of the main opposition group(s). The examples, which vary in their levels of intensity, are too numerous to cite. Governing under such circumstances becomes very difficult with, in many cases, more than half the population not recognizing the credibility of the election results.

3   **Divisive**

One of the most common features of Western-styled multiparty politics is its divisiveness. This has been seen everywhere, and no less so in Africa. Indeed, one of the best strategies of African politicians under the multiparty system is to use ethnicity, region, or religion to divide an electorate in order to advance their cause of winning an election. Stoking these divisional wounds, open and sensitive as they are, with many having histories dating back centuries, can lead, and have led, to anywhere from civil unrest to civil war. Under this system, the belligerence between political adversaries is so intense that it makes it nearly impossible for any significant degree of cooperation or compromise to take place in the interests of the common good.

4   **Destabilizing**

Peace and stability, which have alluded much of Africa during the post-colonial period, are two of the most important prerequisites for development. The critical absence of these two conditions is why the huge number of coup d'états that have taken place across the continent have been so damaging. However, the multiparty system, in effect, can result in as much political destabilization as do the countless coups. Changing the political guard every 4–5 years, which includes removing the institutional memory of senior bureaucrats, would prevent the Union Government of Africa from planning for the long-term development of the continent. Priorities are displaced, while uncertainties and confusion set in, resulting in makeshift, ad hoc solutions concocted to replace programmes that were devised and being managed by persons with the requisite expertise.

In addition to all of the above, the multiparty system has also proven to be a smokescreen for masking class domination and exploitation. Where the multiparty system is practiced, unabashedly, the major parties vying for power serve to defend, wholeheartedly, the capitalist system and its extension, imperialism, despite the animated arguments they have, and nefarious insults they level at each other. Veritably, the Labour and Conservative parties in the UK, and the Democratic and Republican parties in the United States, for example, all represent the vested interests, domestically and globally, of the multimillionaires and multibillionaires of their respective countries. In Africa, the constantly bickering parties vying for political power under the multiparty system represent much the same. Their willingness to oversee, manage, and maintain the neo-colonial grip the Global North has on Africa is exceedingly apparent.

This is why Nkrumah insisted on the one party state for Africa:

> A people's parliamentary democracy, with a one-party system, is better able to express and satisfy the common aspirations of a nation as a whole, than a multi-party parliamentary system, which is in fact only a ruse for perpetuating and covering up the inherent struggle between the 'haves' and the have-nots.'[78]

A one-party state in the hands of a despot, however, can easily evolve into tyrannical rule where the wealth of the nation is siphoned into the pockets of the ruling elite and their neo-colonial masters abroad. This was the case in Zaire under the corrupt, psychotic, embezzler, Mobutu Sese Seko. And there have been many others. Nkrumah, however, was careful to note that the one party state is suited for a socialist society that upholds the sanctity of democratic governance:

> A one-party state can only function for the good of the people within the framework of a socialist state or in the developing state with a socialist programme. The government governs through the people, and not through class cleavages and interests. In other words, the basis of government is the will of the people.[79]

In fact, shortly after colonial rule ended in Ghana, Nkrumah shared his intentions on governance with the entire world: 'We in Africa will evolve forms of government rather different from the traditional Western pattern but no less democratic in their protection of the individual and his inalienable rights.'[80] Even the honourable U Thant, the third Secretary-General of the UN, said much the same in 1962, demonstrating his understanding that democracy is not, by definition, indelibly linked to the multiparty system:

> It is a mistake to assume that the political institutions of the newly independent states will be of the same type as those prevailing in Britain, or that there will necessarily be two main parties competing against each other for the votes of the people. The notion that democracy requires the existence of an organized opposition to the government of the day is not valid. Democracy requires only freedom of opposition, not necessarily its organized existence.[81]

In this regard, perhaps one of the greatest mistakes Africa made at independence was to marginalize and, in most cases, jettison its own precolonial *political* culture. This is a culture that includes many of the basic principles of democracy.[82] Indeed, Athens is no more the birthplace of democracy than it is the birthplace of medicine, astronomy, geometry, architecture, agriculture, or any other major science or philosophy that can be traced, rather, to Africa, the cradle of civilization. Governance is no exception.[83] This is not to suggest that African states should have, at the dawn of independence, instituted their traditional system of chieftaincy as their form of government, especially with its emphasis on *royal* blood ties. Instead, it would have been best if systems of government in Africa during the post-colonial period were derived from, built upon, and carved out of the democratic principles of its political heritage. After all, this heritage was imbued with its own unique cultural patterns in the selection of leaders, separation of powers, checks and balances for protection against abuse, and removal from office of leaders who had gone astray. And not only was it largely democratic, exemplified, to some extent, by the pivotal role played by the Council of Elders; it also included the invaluable contribution of women. Clearly, this would have been infinitely better than copying, blindly, an alien, Western style of government designed to undermine Africa's unity and strength.

With a critical *class* analysis of this heritage, which, by the way, beamed with stability, the masses of African people and their leaders will have to reassert the African Personality in governance by creating a Union Government of Africa that is a democratic expression of the will of its people. This expression can best be represented by a single party, a mass party, that reflects the Pan-African aspirations of Global Africa. However, the mass party is not like the political parties found in the Global North. In the latter case, their primary connection with citizens is to win their votes every 4–5 years by spending hundreds of millions of dollars in election campaigning. The mass party's relationship with its people is entirely different. Farmer cooperatives, women's brigades, youth organizations, cultural troupes, health corps, and various other *organized* sectors of the society are integral parts of the mass party, each playing its part in helping the party shape and meet its goals and objectives in pursuit of the Pan-African imperative. This type of sociopolitical arrangement—formed on the local to the continental level— is far more consistent with Africa's cultural heritage, and will help to ensure the people's full and enthusiastic involvement with the party in all programmes, projects, and policies effecting the nation's future.

Notes

1 Walter Rodney, '*Howe Europe Underdeveloped Africa*,' Dar es-Salaam: Bogle-L'Ouverture Publications, London and Tanzanian Publishing House, 1973, Chapter II; Kwame Nkrumah, 'African Socialism Revisited,' in *Revolutionary Path*, New York: International, 1973, pgs. 438–445.

2 Kwame Nkrumah, ibid., pgs. 440–441.
3 Emmanuel Akyeampong, 'The Contribution of African Women to Economic Growth and Development in Pre-Colonial and Colonial Periods: Historical Perspectives and Policy Implications,' *Economic History of Developing Regions*, Vol. 29, June 2014, retrieved from: https://openknowle dge.worldbank.org/bitstream/handle/10986/6056/WPS6051.pdf?sequence= 1&isAllowed=y.
4 Frantz Fanon was one of the first Pan-Africanists to recognize and write about this phenomenon. See Fanon's *The Wretched of the Earth*, New York, Grove, 1963, especially his chapter titled, 'The Pitfalls of National Consciousness,' pgs. 147–205.
5 Kwame Nkrumah, *Class Struggle in Africa*, New York: International, 1970, pg. 10.
6 'A Tale of Two Continents: Fighting Inequality in Africa,' An Oxfam International Briefing Paper (written by Emma Seery et al.), September 2019, pg. 2, retrieved from: https://oi-files-d8-prod.s3.eu-west-2.amazon aws.com/s3fs-public/file_attachments/bp-tale-of-two-continents-fighting-inequality-africa-030919-en.pdf; Lucas Chancel et al., *Income Inequality in Africa, 1990–2017*, World Income Database (WID), World Issue Brief, September 2019, retrieved from: https://wid.world/document/income-ine quality-in-africa-1990-2017-wid-world-issue-brief-2019-06/#:~:text=Afr ica%20has%20the%20highest%20gap,inequality%20regions%20such%20 as%20the.
7 Kwame Nkrumah, '*Neo-Colonialism: The Last Stage of Imperialism*,' New York: International, 1965.
8 Kwame Nkrumah, op cit.
9 For a better understanding of the derivative relationship between labour and exchange value, see Karl Marx, *Capital: A Critique of Political Economy, Volume I*, edited by Frederick Engels, Vol. 1, Chapter 1, International Publishers: New York, 1967.
10 Rudolf Traub-Merz, 'The African Textile and Clothing Industry: From Import Substitution to Export Orientation,' in Herbert Jauch and Rudolk Traub-Merz, *The Future of the Textile and Clothing Industry in Sub-Saharan Africa*, Bonn: Friedrich-Ebert-Stiftung, 2006, pgs. 9–35; Gumisai Mutume, 'Lost of Textile Markets Cost African Jobs,' Africa Renewal, 2006, retrieved from: www.un.org/africarenewal/magazine/april-2006/loss-textile-market-costs-african-jobs; John Baffes, 'The "Cotton Problems" in West and Central Africa: The Case for Domestic Reforms,' CATO Institute, July 11, 2007, Economic Development Bulletin, No. 11; William G. Moseley and Leslie C. Gray, *Hanging by a Thread: Cotton, Globalization, and Poverty in Africa*, Columbus: Ohio University Press, 2008.
11 Victor Kwawukume, 'Ghana, Cote d'Ivoire Cooperate to Reap Higher Benefits from Global Chocolate Industry,' Graphic Online, October 18, 2017, retrieved from: www.graphic.com.gh/news/general-news/ghana-cote-d-ivoire-cooperate-to-reap-higher-benefits-from-global-cocoa-industry. html; Bridgitte Boakye, 'Why These Two African Countries Produce

60% of the World's Cocoa but Get Only 5% of the $100 Billion Industry,' Face2Face Africa, June 14, 2018, retrieved from: https://face2faceafrica. com/article/why-these-two-african-countries-produce-60-of-the-worlds-cocoa-but-get-only-5-of-the-100-billion-industry.

12 Leanne de Bassom Pierre et al., 'The $US 100b Chocolate Industry's Child Labour Problems Getting Worse,' The Sunday Morning Herald, October 20, 2020, retrieved from: www.smh.com.au/business/the-economy/the-us100b-chocolate-industry-s-child-labour-problem-is-getting-worse-20201020-p566q1. html; Santadarshan Sadhu et al., *NORC Final Report: Assessing Progress in Reducing Child Labour in Cocoa Production in Cocoa Growing Areas in Cote d'Ivoire and Ghana*, October 2020, retrieved from: www.norc.org/PDFs/ Cocoa%20Report/NORC%202020%20Cocoa%20Report_English.pdf.

13 Etsey Atisu, 'Historic Win for Ghana and Cote d'Ivoire After Halting Global Cocoa Sales Until Farmers Get Fair Price,' Face2Face Africa, June 14, 2019, retrieved from: https://face2faceafrica.com/article/historic-win-for-ghana-and-cote-divoire-after-halting-global-cocoa-sales-until-farm ers-get-fair-price.

14 Kwame Nkrumah, *Neo-Colonialism* ... op cit., pg. 11.

15 Anthony Myers, 'Hershey Move to Buy Cocoa on Futures Market Threatens LID Agreement with Ghana and Cote d'Ivoire,' Confectionary News.com, November 23, 2020, retrieved from: www.confectionerynews.com/Article/ 2020/11/23/Hershey-move-of-buying-cocoa-on-futures-market-threatens-LID-agreement-with-Ghana-and-Cote-d-Ivoire; Isis Almeida, 'Hershey Behind Big Cocoa Trade that Upended N.Y. Markets, Bloomberg,' November 20, 2020, retrieved from: www.bloomberg.com/news/articles/2020-11-19/ hershey-is-behind-the-big-cocoa-trade-that-upended-n-y-markets.

16 Susan Bartels et al., 'Militarized Sexual Violence in South Kivu, Democratic Republic of the Congo, *Journal of Interpersonal Violence*,' Vol. 10, No. 10, 2012, pgs. 1–19; Aurelie K. Kassangye et al., 'Sexual Violence at the Eastern Region of the Democratic Republic of the Congo and its Public Health Implications,' *World J Public Health Sciences*, 2014 3(1):11, retrieved from: http://rrpjournals.org/wjphs/en_wjphs_vol_3_iss_1_pg_11_18.pdf.

17 The Guardian, www.theguardian.com/world/2015/may/19/marikana-massacre-untold-story-strike-leader-died-workers-rights.

18 Quoted in *Le Monde*, 16/8/12.

19 *Demanding the Impossible: Platinum Mining Profits and Wage Demands in Context (Abridged Version)*, Andrew Bowman and Gilad Isaacs, RMF, Occasional Policy Paper 11, June 2014.

20 The poor safety record of these platinum mines results, on average, in nearly 200 fatalities each year. See 'Scandals and Strikes: An Uncertain Future for Platinum in South Africa,' Lindsay Dodgson, January 13, 2016, retrieved from: www.mining-technology.com/features/featurescandals-and-strikes-an-uncertain-future-for-platinum-in-south-africa-4744103/; See also 'Super Profits, but Not for Mineworkers,' Sipho Kings, January 6, 2014, Mail and Guardian: Africa's Best Read, retrieved from: http://mg.co.za/article/2014-06-05-super-profits-but-not-for-mineworkers.

21 See 'Unlocking Africa's Agricultural Potential to Create Wealth,' Remarks by Dr. Akinwumi Adesina, President, *African* Development Bank at the Public Lecture of the Food and Agricultural Organization (FAO) of the United Nations, held at the FAO Head Office, Rome, Italy, August 27, 2018, *ADB Group, Newsletter*, retrieve from: www.afdb.org/en/news-and-events/ unlocking-africas-agricultural-potential-to-create-wealth-18437.

22 Dambisa Moyo, *Dead Aid: Why AID Is Not Working and How There is a Better Way for Africa*, New York: Farrar, Straus and Giroux, 2009; Ravi Kanbur, 'Aid, Conditionality, and Debt in Africa,' in Finn Tarp, ed., *Foreign Aid and Development: Lessons Learnt and Directions for the Future*, Routledge, 2000; Shola J. Omotola and Hassan Saliu, 'Foreign Aid, Debt Relief, and African Development: Problems and Prospects,' *South African Journal of International Affairs*, Vol. 16, No. 1, 2009, pgs. 87–102.

23 Marcus Power and Giles Mohan, 'Towards a Critical Geopolitics of China's Engagement with African Development,' Geopolitics, August 20, 2010, pgs. 1–32, retrieved from: (PDF) Towards a Critical Geopolitics of China's Engagement with African Development (researchgate.net).

24 Jong-Dae Parker, *Re-Inventing Africa's Development: Linking Africa to the Korean Development Model*, Cham, Switzerland, Palgrave McMillan, 2019, pgs. 37–41; Andrei Schleifer, 'Peter Bauer and the Failure of Foreign Aid,' *Cato Journal*, Vol. 29, No. 3 (Fall 2009), pgs. 379–382; Kingsley Chiedu Moghalu, *Emerging Africa: How the Global Economy's 'Last Frontier' Can Prosper and Matter*, London: Penguin Books, 2014, pgs. 25–28; Charlie K 'Aid, Governance, and Exploitation,' '*International Socialism: A Quarterly Review of Socialist Theory*,' Summer 2005, retrieved from: http://isj.org. uk/aid-governance-and-exploitation/.

25 Itai Kabonga, 'Dependency Theory and Donor Aid: A Critical Analysis,' *Journal of Development Studies*, Vol. 46, No. 2, August 2017, pg. 10.

26 Nkrumah, *Neo-Colonialism*, op cit., pgs. 242–243; Christina Kingston et al., 'The Impact of the World Bank and IMF Structural Adjustment Programmes on Africa: The Case Study of Cote d'Ivoire, Senegal, Uganda, and Zimbabwe,' *Sacha Journal of Policy and Strategic Studies*, Vol. 1, No. 2, 2011, pgs. 110–130.

27 In 1963 at the first meeting of the Organization of African Unity, in Addis Ababa, each head of state received a personal copy of Nkrumah' classic book, '*Africa Must Unite*,' which had just recently been published.

28 Kate Bayless and Terry McKinley, Privatizing Basic Utilities in Sub-Saharan Africa: The MDG Impact, *Policy Research Brief*, International Poverty Centre/United Nations Development Programme, January 2007, No. 3.

29 Jomo Kwame Sundaram et al., *Globalization and Development in Sub-Saharan Africa, United Nations Publication*, 2011.

30 Karikari Amoa-Gyarteng, 'Depreciation of Ghanaian Currency between 2012 and 2014: Result of Activities of Speculators re Economic Fundamentals,' *American Journal of Economics*, 2016, Vol. 6, No. 6, pgs. 300–305.

31 Thomas Stubbs et al., 'The Impact of IMF Conditionality on Government Health Expenditure: A Cross-national Analysis of 16 West African Nations,' *Social Science and Medicine*, Vol. 174, February 2017, pgs. 220–227; Adel Daoud and Bernhard Reinsburg, 'Structural Adjustment, State Capacity, and Child Health: Evidence from IMF Programmes,' *International Journal of Epidemiology*, Vol. 48, No. 2, April 2019, pgs. 445–454; Vincent Lloyd and Robert Weissman, 'How International Monetary Fund and World Bank Policies Undermine Labor Power and Rights,' *International Journal of Health Services*, Vol. 32, No. 3, July 1, 2002, pgs. 433–442.

32 Kenan Malik, 'As a System, Foreign Aid is a Fraud and Does Nothing for Inequality,' *The Guardian*, September 2, 2018, retrieved from: www. theguardian.com/commentisfree/2018/sep/02/as-a-system-foreign-aid-is-a-fraud-and-does-nothing-for-inequality; Donald Gering, 'Rwanda Demands an End to Tied Aid,' The Guardian, November 28, 2011, retrieved from: www.theguardian.com/global-development/2011/nov/28/busan-deadline-to-end-tied-aid.

33 J.K. Kwakye, *Overcoming Africa's Addiction to Foreign Aid: A Look at Some Financial Engineering to Mobilize Other Sources*, Institute of Economic Affairs, No. 32 IEA Monograph, 2010, pgs. 1–11.

34 Thomas Ayodele et al., 'African Perspectives on AID: Foreign Assistance Will Not Pull Africa Out of Poverty,' *CATO Institute Bulletin*, No. 2, September 14, 2005, pg. 1.

35 Charles Nixon Yeboah, 'Ghana's Debt-to-GDP Ratio Hit 76.7% in 2020 – IMF,' retrieved from: www.myjoyonline.com/ghanas-debt-to-gdp-ratio-to-hit-76-7-in-2020-imf/; Business News, 'Ghana's Foreign Debt Obligation and the Cedi's Value,' Ghanaweb, Friday, February 15, 2019, Source: Goldstreet Business, retrieved from: www.ghanaweb.com/GhanaHomePage/business/Ghana-s-foreign-debt-obligations-and-the-cedi-s-value-723563.

36 Osman Dawelbait, 'Debt Crisis in Africa,' *Journal of Economics and Sustainable Development*, Vol. 6, No. 8, 2015, pgs. 21–29, retrieved from: https://iiste.org/Journals/index.php/JEDS/article/viewFile/21903/22244; Rodney Muhumuza, 'Zambia's Risk of Default Highlights Africa's Debt Crisis,' *The Associated Press*, November 1, 2020, retrieved from: https://apn ews.com/article/virus-outbreak-africa-health-zambia-financial-markets-0a37160eda1b5e0fe822eab8b85f7e26.

37 See Transparency International: The Global Coalition against Corruption: www.transparency.org/en/; Juan Cole, 'Top 10 Ways the United States is the Most Corrupt Country in the World,' *Informed Consent*, January 31, 2019, retrieved from: www.commondreams.org/views/2019/01/31/top-10-ways-united-states-most-corrupt-country-world; Stephen Johnson, 'The Globasol Economy Loses $3.6 Trillion to Corruption Each Year Says UN,' Big Think, December 30, 2018, retrieved from: https://bigthink.com/polit ics-current-affairs/corruption-costs-world-3-6-trillion?rebelltitem=1#rebel ltitem1.

38 Zekeri Momoh, 'Corruption and Governance in Africa,' Proceedings of the International Conference for Sub-Saharan African Transformation and

Development, Vol. 3, No. 6, March 12–13, 2015, retrieved from: file:///C:/Users/Dr.%20Michael%20Williams/Downloads/CORRUPTION_AND_GOVERNANCE_IN_AFRICA.pdf.

39 Zekeri Momoh, 'Globalization and Corruption in Africa,' *Fountain Journal of Management and Social Sciences*, Vol. 4, No. 2, 2015, pgs. 145–158; Jergen Juel Andersen et al., 'Elite Capture of Foreign Aid: Evidence of Offshore Accounts,' Policy Research Paper 9150, World Bank Group, February 18, 2020, retrieved from: http://documents1.worldbank.org/curated/en/493201582052636710/pdf/Elite-Capture-of-Foreign-Aid-Evidence-from-Offshore-Bank-Accounts.pdf.

40 Vanguard, 'Corruption Stalls Uninterrupted Electricity – CIPE,' *Vanguard News*, December 8, 2020, retrieved from: www.vanguardngr.com/2020/12/corruption-stalls-uninterrupted-electricity-to-africa-cipe-2/.

41 Uwagbale Edwrd-Ekpu, 'The World's Largest Rubber Company is Being Blamed Again for Pollution in a Liberian River,' *Quartz Africa*, February 25, 2020; Robtel Neajai Pailey, 'Slavery Ain't Dead, It's Manufactured in Liberia's Rubber,' *Pambazuka News*, April 25, 2007, retrieved from: www.pambazuka.org/global-south/slavery-ain%E2%80%99t-dead-it%E2%80%99s-manufactured-liberia%E2%80%99s-rubber; Tarnue Johnson, *A Critical Examination of Firetsone's Operations in Liberia: A Case Study Approach*, Bloomington, Indiana: Authorhouse, 2010; Moses Uneh Yahmia, 'Liberia: The Firestone Republic,' The Perspective, March 28, 2019, retrieved from: www.theperspective.org/2019/0327201901.php.

42 Re-Define, 'Foreign Direct Investment: A Critical Perspective,' *A Re-Define Working Paper*, February 3, 2007, retrieved from: http://re-define.org/sites/default/files/ForeignDirectInvestment-Acriticalper.pdf; Abhijit Mohanty, 'Uranium in Niger: When a Blessing Becomes a Curse,' Geopolitical Monitor, April 19, 2018; Dale Dewar, 'Uranium Mining: Environmental and Human Health Effects,' in *Nuclear Non-Proliferation in International Law*, Jonathan L. Black-Branch and Dieter Fleck, eds., Vol. IV, pgs. 229–235.

43 Jean-Germain Gros, ' "Big Think," Disjointed Incrementalism: Chinese Economic Success and Policy Lessons for Africa or the Case for Pan-Africanism,' *African Journal of International Affairs*, 2008, Vol. 11, 2, No. 2, pgs. 75–77.

44 Godfred A. Bokpin, 'Foreign Direct Investment and Environmental Sustainability in Africa: The Role of Institutions and Governance,' *Research in International Business and Finance*, Vol. 39, Part A, January 2017, pgs. 239–247; David H. Shinn, 'The Environmental Impact of China's Investment in Africa,' *Cornell International Law Journal*, Vol. 49, No. 25, 2016, pgs. 25–67.

45 Mick Brooks, 'An Introduction to Marx's Labour Theory of Value,' *In Defense of Marxism*, July 12, 2005, retrieved from: www.marxist.com/marx-marxist-labour-theory-value.htm.

46 Fabian Jintae Froese et al., 'Challenges for Foreign Companies in China: Implications for Research and Practice,' *Asian Business and Management*,

2019, Vol. 18, pgs. 249–263; Cory Bennett and Bryan Bender, 'How China Acquires "The Crown Jewels" of US Technology,' *Politico*, May 22, 2018, retrieved from: www.politico.com/story/2018/05/22/china-us-tech-companies-cfius-572413; Sungcheol Lee et al., 'Technology Transfer of Foreign Direct Investment in China,' *Geography*, October 2003, Vol. 88, No. 4, pgs. 289–299.

47 Eric D. Lawrence, 'Fiat Chrysler Names New Leadership in China,' Detroit Free Press, April 29, 2019, retrieved from: www.freep.com/story/money/cars/chrysler/2019/04/29/fiat-chrysler-china-max-trantini/3614821002/; Jeff Spross, 'China's Forced Technology Transfer is Actually a Pretty Good Idea,' *The Week*, April 1, 2019, retrieved from: https://theweek.com/articles/831859/chinas-forced-technology-transfer-actually-pretty-good-idea; For Fiat Chrysler car sales and technology sharing in China see: www.statista.com/statistics/475673/vehicle-sales-of-fca-in-leading-countries/; www.macrotrends.net/stocks/charts/FCAU/fiat-chrysler-automobiles/revenue; www.cnbc.com/2020/01/17/fiat-chrysler-and-foxconn-plan-chinese-electric-vehicle-joint-venture.html.

48 Kwame Nkrumah, *Handbook of Revolutionary Warfare*, New York: International Publishers, 1968, pg. 28.

49 Ibid.

50 Eric Williams, *Capitalism and Slavery*, New York: Capricorn, 1966.

51 V.I. Lenin, *Imperialism: The Highest Stage of Capitalism*, New York: International.

52 Simon Batterbury and Frankline Ndi, 'Land Grabbing in Africa,' In Binns, J.A et al., *The Routledge Handbook on African Development*, London: Routledge, 2018, pgs. 573–582.

53 Alan Maass, *The Case for Socialism*, Chicago, Ill: Haymarket Books, 2010.

54 Kwame Nkrumah, *Handbook of Revolutionary Warfare: A Guide to the Armed Phase of the African Revolution*, New York: International, 1968, pg. 29.

55 Karl Marx and Frederick Engels, *The Manifesto of the Communist Party, in Marx/Engels Selected Works, Vol. 1*, Moscow: Progress Publishers, 1969, pgs. 98–137.

56 R.W. Davies, 'Lenin, Stalin, and the New Economic Policy, 1921–5,' in *Soviet History in the Yeltsin Era: Studies in Russian and East European History and Society*, London: Palgrave Macmillan, 1997, pgs. 135–145.

57 Michael A. Peters, 'The Chinese Dream: Xi Jinping Thought on Socialism with Chinese Characteristics for a New Era,' *Educational Philosophy and Theory*, Vol. 49, No. 14, 2017, pgs. 1304–2017; Yeonsik Choi, 'The Evolution of "Socialism with Chinese Characteristics": Its Elliptical Structure of Socialist Principles and Chinese Realities,' *Pacific Focus: Inha Journal of International Studies*, Vol. 26, No. 3, 2011, pgs. 385–404.

58 Melanie Beresford, '*Doi Moi* in Review: The Challenge of Building Market Socialism in Vietnam,' *Journal of Contemporary Asia*, Vol. 38, No. 2, May 2008, pgs. 221–243; Pietro Masina, 'Vietnam between Developmental State and Neoliberalism: The Case of the Industrial Sector,' In *Developmental*

124   *Class divide and socialism in Africa*

Politics in Transition, C. Kyung-Sup et al., eds., London: Palgrave Macmillan, 2012, pgs. 188–210.

59 C.P. Emenike et al., eds. 'Accessing Safe Drinking Water in Sub-Saharan Africa: Issues and Challenges in South-West Nigeria,' In *Sustainable Cities and Society*, Amsterdam: Elsevier, 2017, pgs. 263–272; African Studies Centre, Leiden, 'Water in Africa,' Retrieved from: www.ascleiden. nl/content/webdossiers/water-africa; Hannah Ritchie and Max Roser, 'Clean Water,' Our World in Data, 2019, Retrieved from: https://ourworl dindata.org/water-access; Danwood M. Chirwa, 'Access to Medicines and Health Care in Sub-Saharan Africa: A Historical Perspective,' *Maryland Journal of International Law*, Vol. 31, No. 1, 2017, pgs. 21–43; Max Roser et al., 'Life Expectancy,' *Our World of Data*, 2019, Retrieved from: https://ourworldindata.org/life-expectancy; Aaron O'Neill, 'Life Expectancy in Africa from 1950 to 2020,' *Statista*, 2019, Retrieved from: www.statista.com/statistics/1076271/life-expectancy-africa-historical/ ; WHO, *Nutrition in the WHO African Region*, World Health Organization, Regional Office for Africa, Brazzaville, 2017; World Bank, The World by Income and Region, World Development Indicators, 2021, Retrieved from: https://datatopics.worldbank.org/world-development-indicators/the-world-by-income-and-region.html.

60 Kwame Nkrumah, *Africa Must Unite*, op cit., pgs.118–131.

61 Ibid., pgs. 120–121.

62 Alex Akurgo, *Kwame Nkrumah: A Story from CIA Files*, Accra: Staricom, 2018; Seymour M. Hersh, 'C.I.A. Said to Have Aided Plotters Who Overthrew Nkrumah in Ghana,' New York Times, May 9, 1978, retrieved from: www.nytimes.com/1978/05/09/archives/cia-said-to-have-aided-plotters-who-overthrew-nkrumah-in-ghana.html.

63 Kwame Nkrumah, *Axioms of Kwame Nkrumah: Freedom Fighter's Edition*, London: Panaf, 1969, pg. 131, in *Handbook of Revolutionary Warfare*, op cit., pg. 91.

64 V.I. Lenin, 'Speech at the First All-Russia Congress of Working Women,' November 19, 1918, Collected Works of V.I. Lenin, Moscow: Progress Publishers, Vol. 28, 1974, pgs. 180–182, retrieved from: www.marxists.org/archive/lenin/works/1918/nov/19.htm.

65 Sékou Touré, *Women in Society*, All-African Women's Revolutionary Union pamphlet, 2006.

66 Quoted in 'Amy Ashwood Garvey: A Revolutionary Pan-African Feminist,' Nydia Sawby, *The Revisionist*, April 1, 2010, retrieved from: https://slcwhb log.com/2010/04/01/amy-ashwood-garvey-a-revolutionary-pan-african-feminist/.

67 Fredoline Anunobi, 'Women and Development in Africa: From Marginalization to Gender Inequality,' *African Social Science Review*, Vol. 2, No. 2, Fall 2002.

68 Urther Rwafa, 'Culture and Religion as Sources of Gender Inequality: Rethinking Challenges Women Face in Contemporary Africa,' *Journal of Literary Studies*, 2016, Vol. 32, No.1, pgs. 43–52.

69 Akosua Adomako Ampofo, 'Gender and Society in Africa: An Introduction,' in *Africa in Contemporary Perspective: A Textbook for Undergraduate Students*, Takyiwaa Manuh and Esi Sutherland-Addy, eds., Accra: Sub-Saharan Publishers, 2013, pgs. 94–115; Takyiwaa Manuh, 'Women and Their Organizations During the Period of CPP Rule in Ghana, 1951–1966,' in *The Life and Work of Kwame Nkrumah*, Trenton: Africa World Press, 1991; Samantha van Schalwyk, *Narrative Landscapes of Female Sexuality in Africa: Collective Stories of Trauma and Transition*, Cham: Palgrave Macmillan, 2018; O.S. Yusuff, 'Gender in Africa,' in *The Development of Africa: Social Indicators Research Series*, J. Adesina and O. Akanle, eds., Vol. 71, Cham: Springer, pgs. 269–288; Michael Kevane, *Women and Development in Africa: How Gender Works*, Boulder, Co: Lynne Rienner, 2014; Toyin Falola et al., eds., *Women, Gender, and Sexualities in Africa*, Durham, NC: Carolina Academic Press, 2013; Catherine M. Cole et al., eds., *Africa After Gender?*, Bloomington, IND: Indiana University Press, 2007.

70 Kwame Nkrumah, 'Speech in the National Assembly,' August 8, 1960, in *Axioms of Kwame Nkrumah*, op cit., pgs. 1–2.

71 Kwame Nkrumah, *Handbook of Revolutionary Warfare*, op cit., pg. 26.

72 Brahima S. Coulibaly and Dhruv Ghandi, 'Mobilization of Tax Revenue in Africa: State of Play and Policy Options,' *African Growth Initiative at Brookings, Policy Brief*, October 2018, retrieved from: www.brookings.edu/wp-content/uploads/2018/10/Mobilization-of-tax-revenues_20181017.pdf.

73 Kwame Nkrumah, *Consciencism: Philosophy and Ideology for Decolonization*, New York: Monthly Review, 1964, pg. 76.

74 Endalcachew Bayeh, 'The Role of Empowering Women and Achieving Gender Equality to the Sustainable Development in Ethiopia,' *Pacific Science Review B: Humanities and Social Sciences*, Vol. 2, No. 1, January 2016, pgs. 37–42; M.N. Chukwu, 'A Study on Gender Involvement in Environmental Protection in Pedro Village, Lagos,' *Academic Journal of Interdisciplinary Studies*, Vol. 3, No. 7, November 2014, pgs. 20–24.

75 Friedrich Engels, *Anti-Duhring*, Progress Publishers: Moscow, 1947, pgs. 323–346; Friedrich Engels, *Socialism: Utopian and Scientific*, Progress Publishers: Moscow, 1974, pgs. 73–74.

76 Kwame Nkrumah, *Axioms*, op cit., pg. 130.

77 Westminster Foundation for Democracy, 'The Cost of Politics in Ghana,' 2017, retrieved from: www.wfd.org/wp-content/uploads/2018/04/Cost_Of_Politics_Ghana.pdf; Abdi Latif Dahir and Yomi Kazeem, 'The Economic Cost of Elections in Africa,' *Business Times: Redefining Business*, March 7, 2019, retrieved from: https://businesstimes.co.zw/the-economic-cost-of-elections-in-africa/; Abdi Latif Dahir, 'Kenya is Set to Hold One of the Most Expensive Elections in Africa,' *Quartz Africa*, July 18, 2017, retrieved from: https://qz.com/africa/1030958/kenyas-elections-will-cost-1-billion-in-government-and-campaign-spend/; Emmanuel Kitamirike and Peter Kisaakye, 'How Much Does it Cost to Run for Office in Uganda?' *Mail and Guardian*, November 3, 2020, retrieved from: https://mg.co.za/africa/2020-11-03-how-much-does-it-cost-to-run-for-office-in-uganda/; Ayo Baje,

'High Costs of Conducting Elections in Nigeria,' The Guardian, February 28, 2019, retrieved from: https://guardian.ng/opinion/high-costs-of-con ducting-elections-in-nigeria/.

78 Kwame Nkrumah, *Consciencism: Philosophy and Ideology for Decolonization*, New York: Monthly Review Press, 1970, pgs. 100–101. See also Nii Ardey Otoo, 'Kwame Nkrumah and the One Party State,' *Nkrumaist Review: Pan-African Perspectives on African Affairs*, Vol. 4, No. 1, June 2008, pgs. 18–21.

79 Kwame Nkrumah, 'Sessional Address to the National Assembly,' February 1, 1966, in *Axioms of Kwame Nkrumah*, op cit., pg. 105.

80 Kwame Nkrumah, 'Speech to the Indian Council on World Affairs,' December 26, 1958, in *Axioms of Kwame Nkrumah*, ibid., pg.103.

81 Quoted in Kwesi Armah, *Africa's Golden Road*, Heinemann: London, 1965, pgs. 78–79.

82 Alexander K.D. Frempong, 'Chieftaincy, Democracy and Human Rights in Pre-Colonial Africa: The Case of the Akan System in Ghana,' in *Chieftaincy in Ghana: Culture, Governance and Development*, Irene K. Odotei and Albert K. Awedoba, eds., Accra: Sub-Saharan Publishers, 2006, pgs. 379–393.

83 Chancellor Williams, *The Destruction of Black Civilization: Great Issues of a Race from 4500 BC to 2000 AD*, Chicago: Third World Press, pgs. 161–175; George C.M. James, *Stolen Legacy*, New York: Classic House Books, 2009; Cheikh Anta Diop, *The African Origins of Civilization: Myth or Reality*, Chicago: Lawrence Hill Book, 1974.

5 Conclusion

Political guidelines on achieving a unified socialist Africa

Much of the Nkrumaist analysis of *how* to achieve a united socialist Africa, the ultimate objective of Pan-Africanism, is encapsulated in one of Nkrumah's most iconic quotes: 'Seek ye first the political kingdom, and all else shall be added unto you.'[1] That the fulfilment of this objective will require a revolutionary transformation of Africa is indubitable. The global interests of finance capital in maintaining the status quo in Africa, inextricably linked with its African mainland alliances, are entrenched, and can only be defeated by revolutionary action across Africa and throughout its diaspora. Revolutionary action, however, results from revolutionary consciousness. This is why Nkrumah placed so much emphasis on the latter: 'The higher the level of a people's political awareness, the greater is their understanding of their historical mission.'[2] However, since he also considered thought without practice to be empty,[3] revolutionary action, in the form of organization, was of paramount importance: 'We must organize as never before because organization determines everything!'[4] This organizational activity must begin, nay, has already begun (over a century ago) with a minority of politically conscious Pan-Africanists in Africa and around the world deciding to organize themselves, globally, in order to achieve the goals and objectives of Pan-Africanism.

Today, the organizational outcome of their efforts, seen in the growth and expansion of *revolutionary* Pan-African organizations in Africa and around the world, is very encouraging.[5] Under the guiding principle of 'No individual person should be without membership in some organization,'[6] the location of *where* this organizational activity takes place in the world is less important than organizers actively pursuing Pan-Africanism as their *primary* objective wherever they are located. Nkrumah argued this point forcefully, entreating his adherents across the African World with one of his most urgent appeals:

DOI: 10.4324/9781003224990-6

> The total liberation and the unification of Africa under an All-African Socialist Government must be the primary objective of all Black revolutionaries throughout the world. It is an objective which, when achieved, will bring about the fulfillment of the aspirations of Africans and people of African descent everywhere. It will at the same time advance the triumph of the international socialist revolution, and the onward progress towards world communism, under which every society is ordered on the principle of –from each according to his ability, to each according to his needs.[7]

Organization, however, is the key. Its benefits are not only universally applicable but, more importantly, no revolutionary change can occur without it. While *reforms* can result from constant *mobilization* of people who are disgruntled over any number of issues, revolutionary change requires revolutionary *organization* to bring it into fruition. Ruling classes cannot be upended, and systems of class, race, and gender oppression cannot be overturned, nor replaced with their opposite, without revolutionary organized resistance as the primary agent of change.

The reasons for this are instructive. First, a people organized synthesizes and multiplies the physical strength and intellectual prowess of individuals exponentially, *ad infinitum*. No individual, no matter how great, no matter how well-intentioned, can match the capabilities of an organized people. Second, organization is best suited to raising the political consciousness of a population, one of the main prerequisites to revolutionary change. Through various means—including the use of leafleting, public rallies, seminars, workshops, demonstrations, marches, and social media—the political education of a population can be raised to a level that will heighten their understanding of, while also lowering their level of tolerance for, injustices being committed against them. In short, their consciousness can be so aroused that they become fed up with an old social order *and* convinced that a new social order is not only preferable but also achievable. Third, as important as it is to *unite* a people against the injustices they endure and for the liberation they seek, it is worth noting that 'unity presupposes organization.'[8] In other words, through the process of political education described earlier, it takes organization to unite a people—their unity being solidly based on a unity of shared ideas, that is, on the ideological principles, goals, and objectives that define the organization. Fourth, organization provides the durability, even permanence, required in the protracted struggle to topple an unjust social order. Based on the pursuit of far-reaching, long-standing, wide sweeping goals and objectives, organizations, also guided by interminable principles, provide themselves with the *raison d'être* for their permanent existence. In short, organizations are built to last, unlike associations or social movements which evolve to address temporary issues, that is, *symptoms* of an unjust social order, for example, increased food prices, police brutality, reduced fuel subsidies, and so on. These issues can be resolved with government reforms, which often results in the dissolution of the association or the social movement once a given issue has been addressed. This is why it is always best for individuals who are, by nature, temporal, to expend their energy in *organizing* for permanent goals and objectives rather than, spontaneously, *mobilizing* for temporary issues. As individuals, we can expire or, through fatigue, simply burn out, making it far better for having expended our energy in building an organization or institution that will survive us. And fifth, organizations can serve as excellent incubators for the training of disciplined and well-informed leaders. This, too, is important because of the fragility and ephemerality of leaders who can either be liquidated or, willy-nilly, decide to abandon the goals and objectives of the organization. It is far more difficult to destroy an organization or to have an organization jettison its core values. As Nkrumah noted years ago:

> Leaders may come and go; they may rise and fall; but the people live on forever, and they can only be joined together by an organization that is active and virile and doing the things for which it was established.[9]

What remains to be done is what has been lacking in the Pan-African movement for decades: the coordination of strategies and tactics of the various Pan-African organizations under one umbrella organization. This would enable each organization, while combining its experiences with others, to become a disciplined part of a single whole, a single organization designed to liberate and unify Africa under a socialist government.[10] The plans for this organizational scheme, based largely in Africa, have been carefully designed by Nkrumah. They are available to be studied, critically, by all students, scholars, and activists interested in revolutionary transformation in Africa.[11] However, they should not be seen as an effort on Nkrumah's part to devise an immutable blueprint designed for all circumstances, insulated from the vicissitudes of space and time. Instead, they are to serve as a guide to action, navigated by one underlying strategic imperative, viz., that Pan-Africanist organizers, especially those active on the mainland, think and act continentally, and not solely within the confines of their separate neo-colonial enclaves:

> The dimension of our struggle is equal to the size of the African continent itself. It is in no way confined within any of the absurd limits of the micro-states created by the colonial powers, and jealously guarded by imperialist puppets during the neo-colonialist period.[12]

In order to challenge and ultimately dismantle neo-colonialist rule in Africa, Pan-Africanist organizers will have to busy themselves with gaining the sympathies, enlisting the support, and recruiting militants from the broad masses of African people. This work is as arduous as it is mundane, yet an absolutely necessity for the transformation of lives. Among the global population of 1.5 billion Africans, including the 1.3 billion living in Africa and the 200 million scattered abroad, the sectors most likely to respond favourably, and be won over to revolutionary Pan-Africanism, include: rural workers (including scantly paid farm labourers and small-scale farmers), industrial mine workers, factory and plant workers, and certain progressive elements among the bourgeoisie (including the petty bourgeoisie, the bureaucratic bourgeoisie, and certain elements of the intelligentsia).[13] Special attention will also have to be given to the revolutionary potential of women, whose contributions to Pan-Africanism, though largely ignored, have been outstanding,[14] and to the youth, especially among university students.[15] In the former case, much has already been said earlier: no revolution can succeed without their full participation; in the latter case, students, when aligned with workers, can 'paralyze a reactionary power structure and compel change.'[16] What will be needed, overall, is a critical assessment of each sector within the context of the nation-state and regional conditions which shape their status and readiness for revolution.[17] Nkrumah has categorized these conditions, effectively, into three major (self-explanatory) regional spheres: Enemy Held Zones, Contested Zones, and Liberated Areas.[18] The assessments—based largely on the level of socio-economic development of the society at-large, the degree of political consciousness of the workers, and the scale of anti-imperialist organizational activity—should inform organizers of the most propitious groups, and their locales, to concentrate on in recruiting Pan-African militants.

Once these assessments are made, the method of struggle in each area will have to be decided. From civil disobedience to armed struggle, from electoral politics to revolutionary warfare, only one set of factors should matter when deciding on the most appropriate means of battle: 'The various methods of our struggle, and the changing from one method to another, should be determined mainly by the circumstances and the set of conditions prevailing in a given territory.'[19] Within this context, the question of violence takes on an entirely different meaning than how liberal pundits often define (and deride) it. Violence, by definition, is synonymous with damage and destruction. Hence, when a child goes hungry in a land of plenty, violence is committed against that child.[20] Thus, the only real issue for revolutionary Pan-Africanists when deciding to go into battle with an adversary as violent as the Global North (and the local allies it weaponizes) is the strategic question of how *reactionary* violence can be defeated by *revolutionary* violence, that is, how the systemic damage and destruction directed against the masses of the people can be eliminated by the damage and destruction directed against systems of exploitation, oppression, and degradation. Nkrumah simplified it best: 'Reactionary violence must be met with revolutionary violence. The latter is employed every time the oppressed take action to end their oppression, whether or not they actually resort to armed struggle.'[21]

In sum, the goals and objectives of Pan-Africanism, along with the strategic means to achieving them, have evolved over centuries. They have emanated from the material struggles and ideological longings of the masses of African people, those at home and those abroad. An appreciation of this reality, elucidated so accurately in the writings and speeches of Kwame Nkrumah, is what defines the Pan-African imperative.

Notes

1 Kwame Nkrumah, *I Speak of Freedom*, London: Heinemann, 1961, pg. xiv.
2 Kwame Nkrumah, *Dark Days in Ghana*, New York: International Publishers, 1968, pg. 158.
3 Kwame Nkrumah, *Consciencism: Philosophy and Ideology of Decolonization*, New York: Monthly Review, 1964, pg. 78.
4 Kwame Nkrumah, 'Organize! Organize! Organize!' Accra Evening News, Editorial, January 14, 1949, in *Revolutionary Path*, Kwame Nkrumah, New York: International, 1973, pg. 77.
5 Below is a partial list of some of these organizations, some of whom have become full-fledged political parties, vying for state power in the various nation-states they are based, all of whom have their own websites explaining their goals, objectives, and programmatic activities: Zimbabwe Movement of Pan-African Socialists (ZIMOPAS); World Wide Pan-African Movement (WWPAM); Pan-African Revolutionary Socialist Party (PRSP); Azania

People's Organization (AZAPO); Afrika Global Network (AGN); Socialist Party of Azania (SOPA); Horn of Africa Pan-Africans for Liberation and Solidarity (PALS); Pan-Africanist Congress of Azania (PAC); All-African Revolutionary Unification Party (A-APRUP); Cincinnati Pan-Afrikan Coalition (CPAC); Socialist Movement of Ghana (SMG); African Party for the Independence of Guinea and Cape Verde (PAIGC); Economic Freedom Fighters (EFF); Liberation Movement Kenya (LMK); And-Jëf/ Revolutionary Movement for New Democracy (AND-JEF); Economic Fighters League (EFL); Pan-African Community Action (PACA); Neo Black Movement of African (NBMA); Revolutionary Socialist League of Kenya (RSL); Amilcar Cabral Ideological School (ACIS); Alliances for Africa (AFA); Pan-African Federalist Movement of North America (PAFM); and All-African People's Revolutionary Party (A-APRP).

6 Kwame Nkrumah, *Revolutionary Path*, op cit., pg. 77.
7 Kwame Nkrumah, *Class Struggle in Africa*, New York: International, 1970, pg. 88.
8 Kwame Nkrumah, 'Never Relax Your Efforts,' *Accra Evening News*, Editorial, May 18, 1949, in *Revolutionary Path*, op cit., pgs. 80–81.
9 Ibid.
10 Kwame Nkrumah, *Handbook of Revolutionary Warfare: A Guide to the Armed Phase of the African Revolution*, New York: International, 1968, pgs. 42–43.
11 Ibid.
12 Ibid., pg. 43.
13 Ibid., pgs. 75–93.
14 Prime News Ghana, 'Pan-Africanism, Women's Rights, and Socialist Development,' September 2, 2016, retrieved from: www.primenewsghana. com/features/pan-africanism-women-s-rights-and-socialist-development. html; Feminist Africa, *Pan-Africanism and Feminism*, No. 19, September 2014, Gender Institute, University of Cape Town; Michael Williams, 'Unsung Heroines of Pan-Africanism: A Preliminary Assessment,' *Abafazi: The Simmons College Review of Women of African Descent,'* Vol. 1, No. 3, Fall 1992, pgs. 3–9.
15 *Handbook of Revolutionary Warfare*, ibid., pgs. 88–89.
16 Ibid., pg. 88.
17 Ibid., pg. 61.
18 Ibid., pgs. 43–50.
19 Ibid., pgs. 49–50.
20 *Revolutionary Path*, op cit., pg. 87.
21 Ibid.

Select bibliography

Books

Biney, Ama. 2011. *The Political and Social Thought of Kwame Nkrumah*. London: Palgrave Macmillan.

Blein, Roger, et al. 2013. *Agriculture in Africa: Transformation and Outlook*. Johannesburg: NEPAD.

Campbell, Horace. 2013. *Global NATO and the Catastrophic Failure in Libya*. New York, NY: Monthly Review.

Campbell, James T. 2006. *Middle Passages: African American Journeys to Africa, 1787–2005*. London: Penguin.

Carmichael, Stokely. 1971. *Stokely Speaks: Black Power Back to Pan-Africanism*. New York, NY: Random House.

Clarke, John Herik. 1974. *Marcus Garvey and the Vision of Africa*. New York, NY: Vintage.

Clarke, John Herik. 2011. *Christopher Columbus and the Afrikan Holocaust: Slavery and the Rise of European Capitalism*. Hunlock, PA: Eworld.

Diop, Cheik Anta. 1974. *The African Origins of Civilization: Myth or Reality*. Chicago, IL: Lawrence Hill Book.

Diop, Cheik Anta. 1989. *The Cultural Unity of Black Africa: The Domains of Patriarchy and of Matriarchy in Classical Antiquity*. London: Karnak House.

Du Bois, W.E.B. 1965. *The World and Africa: An Inquiry into the Part Which Africa Has Played in World History*. New York, NY: International.

Du Bois, W.E.B. 1970. *The Negro*. London: Oxford.

Fanon, Frantz. 1963. *The Wretched of the Earth*. New York, NY: Grove.

Fanon, Frantz. 1967. *Black Skin, White Masks*. New York, NY: Grove.

Fanon, Frantz. 1967. *Toward the African Revolution*. New York, NY: Grove.

Garvey, Amy Jacques. 1970. *Garvey and Garveyism*. New York, NY: Collier-Macmillan.

Garvey, Marcus. 1967. *The Philosophy and Opinions of Marcus Garvey or Africa for the Africans*. London: Frank Cass.

Grant, Colin. 2008. *Negro with a Hat: The Rise and Fall of Marcus Garvey*. London: Vintage.

Gros, Jean-Germain. 2014. *Healthcare Policy in Africa: Institutions and Politics from Colonialism to the Present*. New York, NY: Rowman & Littlefield.

Horne, Gerald. 2000. *Race Woman: The Lives of Shirley Graham Du Bois*. New York, NY: NYU Press.

James, C.L.R. 1963. *The Black Jacobins: Toussaint L'Ouverture and the San Domingo Revolution*. New York, NY: Vintage.

James, C.L.R. 1969. *History of Pan-African Revolt*. Washington, DC: Drum and Spear.

James, C.L.R. 1977. *Nkrumah and the Ghana Revolution*. Westport, CT: Lawrence Hill.

Lenin, V.I. 1939. *Imperialism: The Highest Stage of Capitalism*. New York, NY: International.

Maass, Alan. 2010. *The Case for Socialism*. Chicago, IL: Haymarket Books.

Malcolm X. 1965. *Malcolm X Speaks*. New York, NY: Grove.

Malcolm X. 1968. *The Speeches of the Malcolm X at Harvard*. New York, NY: Morrow.

Malcolm X. 1970. *By Any Means Necessary*. New York, NY: Pathfinder.

Martin, Tony. 1976. *Race First: The Ideological and Organizational Struggles of Marcus Garvey and the Universal Negro Improvement Association*. Westport, CT: Greenwood.

Martin, Tony. 1983. *The Pan-African Connection: From Slavery to Garvey and Beyond*, Dover, MA: The Majority Press.

Martin, Tony. 2000. *Amy Ashwood Garvey, Pan-Africanist, Feminist and Mrs. Marcus Garvey No. 1, Or, A Tale of Two Amies*, Dover, MA: Majority Press.

Mathurin, Owen Charles. 1976. *Henry Sylvester Williams and the Origins of the Pan-African Movement, 1869–1911*. Westport, CT: Greenwood.

M'buyinga, Elenga. 1982. *Pan-Africanism or Neo-Colonialism?: The Bankruptcy of the O.A.U.* London: Zed.

Nkrumah, Kwame. 1957. *Ghana: The Autobiography of Kwame Nkrumah*. New York, NY: International.

Nkrumah, Kwame. 1961. *I Speak of Freedom*. London: Heinemann.

Nkrumah, Kwame. 1962. *Towards Colonial Freedom*. London: Heinemann.

Nkrumah, Kwame. 1963. *Africa Must Unite*. New York, NY: International.

Nkrumah, Kwame. 1964. *Consciencism: Philosophy and Ideology for Decolonization*. New York, NY: Monthly.

Nkrumah, Kwame. 1965. *Neo-Colonialism: The Last Stage of Imperialism*. New York, NY: International.

Nkrumah, Kwame. 1967. *Axioms of Kwame Nkrumah: Freedom Fighter's Edition*. New York, NY: International.

Nkrumah, Kwame.1967. *Challenge of the Congo: A Case Study of Foreign Pressures in an Independent State*. New York, NY: International.

Nkrumah, Kwame. 1967. *Voice from Conakry*. London: Panaf.

Nkrumah, Kwame. 1968. *Dark Days in Ghana*. New York, NY: International.

Nkrumah, Kwame. 1968. *Handbook of Revolutionary Warfare: A Guide to the Armed Phase of the African Revolution*. New York, NY: International.

Nkrumah, Kwame. 1968. *The Struggle Continues*. London: Panaf.

Nkrumah, Kwame. 1970. *Class Struggle in Africa*. New York, NY: International.
Nkrumah, Kwame. 1973. *Revolutionary Path*. New York, NY: International.
Nkrumah, Kwame. 1974. *Rhodesia File*. London: Zed Books.
Nyerere, Julius. 1962. *Ujamaa: Essays in Socialism*. New York, NY: Oxford.
Obeng, Samuel. 1979. *Selected Speeches of Kwame Nkrumah*, Vol. 1. Accra: Afram.
Obeng, Samuel. 1979. *Selected Speeches of Kwame Nkrumah*, Vol. 2. Accra: Afram.
Obeng, Samuel. 1997. *Selected Speeches of Kwame Nkrumah*, Vol. 3. Accra: Afram.
Obeng, Samuel. 1997. *Selected Speeches of Kwame Nkrumah*, Vol. 4. Accra: Afram.
Obeng, Samuel. 1997. *Selected Speeches of Kwame Nkrumah*, Vol. 5. Accra: Afram.
Padmore, George. 1931. *The Life and Struggle of Negro Toilers*. London: Red International of Labor Unions.
Padmore, George. 1972. *Pan-Africanism or Communism*. Garden City, NY: Doubleday.
Poe, D. Zizwe. 2011. *Kwame Nkrumah's Contribution to Pan-Africanism: An Afrocentric Analysis*. London: Routledge.
Ransby, Barbara. 2013. *Eslanda: The Large and Unconventional Life of Mrs. Paul Robeson*. New Haven, CT: Yale University Press.
Rodney, Walter. 1974. *How Europe Underdeveloped Africa*. Washington, DC: Howard.
Schalwyk, Samantha van. 2018 *Narrative Landscapes of Female Sexuality in Africa: Collective Stories of Trauma and Transition*. Cham: Palgrave Macmillan.
Touré, Sékou. 1962. *The International Policy and Diplomatic Action of the Democratic Party of Guinea*. Cairo: S.O.P.
Touré, Sékou. 1977. *Strategy and Tactics of the Revolution*. Conakry: Press Office.
Touré, Sékou. 1980. *The United States of Africa*. Guinea: Imprimerie Nationale Patrice Lumumba.
Williams, Michael. 1992. *Pan-Africanism: An Annotated Bibliography*. Pasadena, CA: Salem.

Articles

Asafu-Adjaye, John. 2014. "The Economic Impacts of Climate Change on Agriculture in Africa," *Journal of African Economies*, Vol. 23, Issue suppl_2, August, pgs. ii17–ii49.
Beresford, Melanie. 2008. "*Doi Moi* in Review: The Challenge of Building Market Socialism in Vietnam," *Journal of Contemporary Asia*, Vol. 38, No. 2, pgs. 221–243.
Faye, Michael L. 2004. "The Challenges Facing Landlocked Developing Countries." *Journal of Human Development*, Vol. 5, No. 1. pgs. 31–68.

Gros, Jean-Germain, 2008. ' "Big Think," Disjointed Incrementalism: Chinese Economic Success and Policy Lessons for Africa or the Case for Pan-Africanism,' *African Journal of International Affairs,*' Vol. 11, No. 2, pgs. 55–87.

Lanshime, Cletus A. 2016. "African Traditional Systems of Conflict Resolution," *The African Anthropologist*, Vol. 20, Nos. 1 and 2, pgs. 262–291.

Moti, Ukertor Gabriel. 2019 "Africa's Natural Resource Wealth: A Paradox of Plenty and Poverty." *Advances in Social Sciences Research Journal*, Vol. 6, No. 7, July, pgs. 483–504.

Rwafa, Urther Rwafa. 2016. "Culture and Religion as Sources of Gender Inequality: Rethinking Challenges Women Face in Contemporary Africa." *Journal of Literary Studies*, Vol. 32, No. 1, pgs. 43–52.

Shulika, Lukong Stella. 2016. "Women and Peace Building: From Historical to Contemporary African Perspectives," *Ubuntu: Journal of Conflict and Social Transformation,* Vol. 5, No. 1, pgs. 7–31.

Touré, Sékou. 1973. "A Dialectical Approach to Culture," in *Contemporary Black Thought: The Best from the Black Scholar.* Robert Chrisman and Nathan Hare (eds). Indianapolis: Bobbs Merrill, pgs. 3–15.

Williams, Michael W. 1983. "Marcus Garvey and Kwame Nkrumah: A Case of Ideological Assimilation, Advancement and Refinement." *Western Journal of Black Studies*, Vol. 7 (Summer), pgs. 94–102.

Williams, Michael W. 1992. 'Unsung Heroines of Pan-Africanism: A Preliminary Assessment,' *Abafazi: The Simmons College Review of Women of African Descent,*' Vol. 3, No. 1, Fall, pgs. 3–9.

Index

African Continental Free Trade Area (AfCFTA) 62, 79–80
African unity: African personality 76–8; bargaining power 63–4; common currency 64–6; conflict resolution 73–5; continental planning 66–72; investment capital 59–61; market size 61–2; military defense 75–6; ocean access 72–3; protectionism 62–3; resources 51–9
African Union (AU) 28, 78–80
AFRICOM 29, 76
agricultural potential 54–5, 66–8
All-African People's Revolutionary Party (A-APRP) 25, 27

biodiversity 70–2
Black Power movement 24
Blyden, Edward Wilmot 10–11

Campbell, Robert 11
Chilembwe, John 14
class exploitation: as aid 97–102; defined 91–3; as investment 102–4; as trade 93–6
Cuffe, Paul 9–10

Delaney, Martin 10
diaspora 8–21, 24–30, 58–9
Du Bois, W.E.B. 6, 14, 18, 21, 37–46

ECOMOG 74–5

Fanon, Frantz 6, 22, 37–46
freshwater availability 55–6

Garnet, Henry Highland 11
Garvey, Amy Ashwood 17
Garvey, Amy Jacques 17, 37–46
Garvey, Marcus 6, 15–16; and socialism and class struggle 40–1
Garvey movement 15–17

Haiti 11–12
Hayford, J.E. Casely 11, 14
health 70
human resources 57–9

industry 68–70

James, C.L.R. 6, 19, 25, 37–46

Malcom X 5, 21, 24, 37–46
mineral wealth 52–4

Nkrumaism 25; and definition 36–7; dialectical materialism 44–5; gender 45–6, 109–11; nationalism 38–40; socialism 40–4
Nyerere, Julius 6, 22, 37–46

Organization of African Unity (OAU) 23, 28
organizational strategy 127–31

Padmore, George 6, 19, 21, 36–46
pan-Africanism: definition 5–7; early emigration efforts 8–13; early

twentieth-century developments
13–19; the new millennium 28–30;
origin 7–8; post-WWII trends
20–8; Western Europe activities
17–19

Qadhafi, Muammar 28–9, 55,
74

renewable energy 56–7

Sam, Chief Alfred 13
socialism: defined 104–6; distribution
of wealth 111–12; environmental
protection 112–13; gender
109–11; governance 113–17;
transitional 106–18

Touré, Ahmed Sékou 6, 25, 37–46
Turner, Henry McNeal 12–13
Ture, Kwame 24–5, 27, 38, 42–3

For Product Safety Concerns and Information please contact our EU
representative GPSR@taylorandfrancis.com
Taylor & Francis Verlag GmbH, Kaufingerstraße 24, 80331 München, Germany

www.ingramcontent.com/pod-product-compliance
Lightning Source LLC
Chambersburg PA
CBHW061256220326
41599CB00028B/5674